Dragons
Led By
Poodles

DRAGONS
LED BY
POODLES

THE INSIDE STORY OF A
NEW LABOUR STITCH-UP

BY

PAUL FLYNN MP

First published in Great Britain 1999
Published by Politico's Publishing
8 Artillery Row
Westminster
London
SW1P 1RZ

Tel 020 7931 0090
Fax 020 7828 8111
Email politicos@artillery-row.demon.co.uk
Website http://www.politicos.co.uk

First Published in Paperback 1999

A catalogue record of this book is available from the British Library.

ISBN 1902301242

Printed and bound in Great Britain by St. Edmundsbury Press.
Cover Design by Advantage
Cover Illustration by Mumph

Dedicated
To all those whose lives
were damaged by
the Stitch-ups.

CONTENTS

INTRODUCTION.

THANKS to Andrew Jeffries, Tony Lynes, Sam Flynn, Rekha Kodikara and Neil Todd who read the manuscript and suggested many improvements. The hundreds of surfers who e-mailed their views have refined the message and revealed new horrors about the Stitch-ups. The best reward for all our work will be a major reform of the Labour Party in Wales and a recognition of the damaging excesses of New Labour.

Paul Flynn
October 1999

FOREWORD

Bob Marshall Andrews MP

Few political labels are more likely to mislead the consumer than the "Electoral College". It has a subtle resonance calculated to promote confidence. It embraces and yokes together the spring of democracy (election) and the fire of intellectual integrity (college). It is a benign metaphor, civilised realpolitik. For precisely this reason it is almost always an instrument of political fraud.

In this fine, literate and engrossing polemic Paul Flynn dissects the lamentable history of New Labour's role in the birth of the Welsh Assembly. It is a chronicle of tragedy in the finest Greek tradition. Good men both—Alun Michael and Rhodri Morgan—locked in a contest for leadership rendered bitter and totally discredited by the corrupting forces of crude political manipulation and fix. At the end the stage is littered with the corpses of the blameless. Fine Labour Assembly candidates unthinkably crushed in the very heartlands of the Labour movement. Islwyn, Llanelli, Rhonnda: all gone as party and people vented their contempt on New Labour's soiled gaberdene. And it may well be terminal. In the European elections that followed Labour MEPs dropped from five to two and Plaid Cymru took 30% of the Welsh vote. The period between the two elections is summarised by the author with the fine, sparse prose and angry integrity that is the hallmark of the man and book:

> *The Party in Wales was now a basket case*
>
> *We had spent nine months in hell and were assailed by guilt, self doubt and insecurity. The safest seats had been lost. Some of our best friends were now enemies. Lost and disorientated, we were marooned in the middle of another election campaign.*

3

The scrupulous quantity of detail assembled from a range of sources across Government and Party reveal not only the strength of the indictment but the cynical and brazen nature of the crime. If allowed to use the elementary democratic process—one man (or woman), one vote—the Welsh Labour party would have elected Rhodri Morgan to lead Wales, a prediction totally vindicated by the one third of the electoral college comprised of members (Michael 35.6: Morgan 64.4).

This transparent and clear verdict was precisely reversed by the union vote (Michael 64: Morgan 36.) With the honourable exceptions (Unison) the main unions failed to ballot their own members or did so with great secrecy. The whole of the TGWU vote (5.1% of the total) was cast by the Union boss George Wright for Alun Michael. There was no official ballot of members. An independemnt poll by Harris showed Morgan 70: Michael 30. The Author says it all.

> *George Wright had not attempted to achieve even the North Korean mockery of democracy. In his case it was not one member one vote but one member 53,000 votes. They were all added to Alun's swelling rotten boroughs pile from the Fixers and Riggers Union.*

Seldom can political fraud have been committed with such swaggering indifference to both guilt or consequence.

The irony implicit in the figures was lost on no one. New Labour's shiny spotless High Command in its first offensive against its own people had, as a last resort, used the mustard gas.

This book may yet do a great service. No doubt it will be vilified as both partisan and disloyal. No doubt its fine iconoclastic wit will be branded as superficial by a political establishment collectively endowed with a plodding mind. None of this will hide its central truth. This Labour Administration has many virtues but one fatal tragic flaw. All Governments ultimately fall on their own swords and the weapon that hangs in the scabbard of New Labour was forged in the obsession with political control at any price.

Labour will shortly vote for its candidate for London Mayor. The curtain is about to rise. The chorus has already announced, yes, an electoral college. Dread the final act.

TRUTH BEFORE RECONCILIATION

'An event has happened, upon which it is difficult to speak and impossible to be silent'

Edmund Burke.

Only the future is certain: the past is always changing.

Even the recent history of the Welsh Labour Party is being falsified. The spinners are trying to obscure the painful truth under layers of gossamer fiction.

All the events described here took place during the past twelve months. It started on a wet Monday night in October 1998 when the Secretary of State for Wales, Ron Davies, took a walk on Clapham Common. It resulted in unimaginable electoral disaster for the Labour Party in Wales. New Labour, with the collaboration of some Old Labour allies in Wales, stitched-up the choice of Ron's replacement. The Party descended into bitter warfare. For the first time in our history, Labour's loyal supporters judged their Party to be unprincipled. They punished the perpetrators of the stitch-up by an electoral cull in some of the safest Labour's seats in Britain.

This is a story of good people behaving badly. The stitch-ups were ruthless. Some had benign intentions but employed foul methods. Most were malign in means and ends. Sometimes new rules were invented, in other cases rules were changed in the middle of the game. The purpose of this book is to record the events before memory fades or spin doctoring distorts. What happened in Wales may be repeated elsewhere in the the UK.

The story was published in a new and, as far as I know, a unique way. Tentatively, it's called ' guest writing ' until a better idea comes along. Some selected chapters were posted on my web-site on the 15th September 1999. I invited readers/surfers to contribute to its writing. Much of what I had written was influenced by my own subjective views and my support for Rhodri Morgan. I asked if it was a fair account?

On the first day, 15,000 hits on the site were recorded. Within three days the total passed 33,000. The media gave it wall to wall coverage and a shoal of e-mails and letters flooded in. Newsrooms I visited were littered with downloaded pages and pictures from the web version. All Welsh newspapers give the embryo book generous and provocative attention.

Here was a a chance for Alun Michael's supporters to state their case. I sent Alun a hard copy of the text. Nothing has been heard from him. Readers outside of Wales may ask if one side committed all the sins while the other was blameless. Although unlikely, that is what happened. It was game played according to the rules by Rhodri's amateurs. Alun's team fielded three times as many players (including professionals), wrote a new rule book to suit their interests, broke most of the game's laws, committed every known foul and then invented a few new ones. They ordered the referee to re-write the rule book during the game. When the match was over they created new laws to ban a re-play.

Dragons and Poodles are beguiling beasts with powerfully delineated attributes. It was inevitable that the the message of the web edition was eclipsed by the characteristics that I have bestowed on my fellow politicians. Images of flaming dragons and pompomed poodles are contagiously seductive. They illuminate the mind and arouse emotions.

A few accusations were made that this book will reopen old wounds. But those injuries have not healed. They were mortal for the political lives of some of our candidates and aspirant candidates. The damage to the perception of the Labour Party is profound. Other books will be published that will probably cast harsher judgments on Labour's self mutilation in Wales. New technology and the constant stream of revelations will ensure that recording this story is a continuing process not the single event of this book of instant history.

Of the many letters I received, this one from Llandaff North in Cardiff spoke for many thousands:

'I am a 64 years old Labour Voter all my life, just like my parents. I will never vote again because of the way Mr Morgan was carved up by the Unions and members of your Party. I do not care who won. All I wanted to see was fair play. I cringe every time I hear Mr Michael

speak. My wife and I are non-voters till we die.'

Traditional Labour voters will not absolve us of guilt until the Labour Party in Wales confronts the truth and resolves to restore our good name. The Bournemouth Conference was awash with appeals to put this last year behind us, to mask the pain with the sedative of amnesia. But there must be a period of honest ventilation before the healing begins. It will not work unless the full lesson has been learnt. Guilt, like grief, can be buried only at the cost of greater problems in future.

In an attempt to define the instincts that shaped the stitch-ups, fifteen precepts of Pompomism have been promulgated. One was contributed by e-mail, and reads, 'Election Cheating is no Gamble: History is Written by Winners'. That must not be allowed to happen. The Party controllers have apparently not learnt the lesson. They may well engineer other stitch-ups. There will be future internal elections in the party. Stitching-up must not become endemic. The compelling message from Wales and Scotland is 'Voters reward those that New Labour cheats'. Millbank should burn the midnight electricity studying the election results achieved by the expelled Dennis Canavan and the ill-used Rhodri Morgan. If the candidate for Mayor of London and other future contests are seen to lack legitimacy in the same way that Alun Michael was, the voters may again punish Labour.

A poll taken in London in September 1999 produced a remarkably similar result to the pre-Assembly poll in Wales which suggested that a Labour Party led by Rhodri would have gained 9% more votes than one led by his New Labour rival, Alun. Ken Livingstone is 12% ahead of his nearest rival in London. A New Labour stitch-up of Ken could serve to catapult him to the top of the poll in the style of Rhodri and Dennis Canavan. A journalist told me that he had been assured by a Millbank official that Ken Livingstone would be barred from the selection process for the Mayor of London unless the party was certain that he would not be chosen as candidate by members of the Party in London.

The other predictable moan was that now was the wrong time to raise these issues. A few weeks after Labour were elected in 1997, I was invited inside 10 Downing Street for the first time ever. It promised to be a joyous event. After 18 years we had done it. Yaroo! What a day for a celebration!

But Tony Blair could not even manage one half-hearted cheer. He lectured us on the failures of past Labour governments and warned against complacency and splits. It was all down-beat and dreary.

Two years into government, the same sour message was the least uplifting ingredient of Tony's otherwise, inspiring Conference speech at Bournemouth.

The shared fury at the stitch-up was bottled up during the two elections in Wales after the February 20th fixed 'election' of Alun Michael as Labour's nomination to be the Assembly's First Secretary. The rule seems to be this. There must be no whisper of dissent after an election or in mid-term or before an election, or before a Conference, or during a Conference and especially after a Conference. Must our mouths be permanently bandaged? The Autumn of 1999 is two years distant from any election. There is no better time to put our party in order.

Not to tell the truth about the Stitch-up is to collaborate with it.

DRAMATIS PERSONAE

Dragons or poodles?

THE political stage is inhabited with fascinating, peculiar people. The characters of this sad drama are a blend of idealism, ambition, high ability and low cunning. There are no heroes or villains. As an instant guide especially to readers outside of Wales, their traits are assessed by their affinities to the characters of dragons and poodles.

Archetypical fierce dragons are awarded five 'flames'; the most subservient poodles get five 'wagging pompoms'. Most are hybrids, a fusion of both beasts. Ratings are determined by permanent traits plus recent conduct in the stitch-ups.

These ratings have been carefully reappraised following persuasive submissions received through the web.

ALUN MICHAEL

Ex-journalist, ex-youth worker, incurable do-gooder. High on detail, low on humour. Earnest, serial father (five children), predictable, irrationally ambitious, is to the Welsh Language what John Prescott is to English. Disillusioned with journalism, he took a job in youth work at half his previous salary. Quick to come to the boil, tetchy when provoked, Pontiff of workalholicism, marathon runner, Tony Blair groupie. At ease with the World of Wales which is evolving in his image.

RATING: *One flame: three pompoms.*

RHODRI MORGAN

Unique political phenomenon. Ideas jokes and solutions Catherine-wheel off in a shower of iridescent brilliance. To Tony Blair, he is an unguided rocket, too unpredictable, too Welsh, too untidy, too original and far too clever. A resourceful and successful Shadow Minister on energy and Wales, ageism denied him Minister's job in 1997. Loves: rugby; beer; anecdotes; marathon running; dolphins; 'True Labour'; wood carving; and his caravan in Mwnt. Hates: tedium; spin doctors; Cardiff Bay. Was 'runner-up to Michael, not a loser'. Possesses fully operational, non-lobotomised brain.

RATING: *Five flames.*

RON DAVIES

One of the most significant Welsh politicians of the century, has achieved what generations of his predecessors failed to deliver. Great political gifts, was moderniser to semi-corrupt 'Labourism' Welsh Local Councils in the 70's. Complex, secretive, astute, passionate on animal welfare and environmental issues, expert on agriculture. Wrenched devolution from the the centralising forces of New Labour with skill and persistence but harmed his reputation by about-turn on devolution referendum. Described Prince Charles as a 'pillock'. Suffered a year of hell, partly self-inflicted; rehabilitation now under way.

RATING: *Five flames: one pompom.*

JON OWEN JONES

Ex-teacher, married to Alison, three young children. Unlikely choice in 1987 of the then seriously deranged constituency Labour Party of Cardiff Central as the non-Militant Tendency candidate. Long serving, long silent whip, pitchforked into Minister's role after sacking of Win Griffiths. Became the team fall guy at the Welsh Office, stayed neutral in Alun - Rhodri scrap, dropped as Minister in July 1999 as part of the Blair Devo-droop push. Looking forward to life as backbencher and applying his expert knowledge of science and education. Appalled vested interests with intelligent NHS speech. Welsh speaking, anti-Democratic Centralism, pro-devolution.

RATING: *Three flames: one pompom.*

PETER HAIN

Sixties' icon, a serial campaigner of distinction and success since 1969. Has tiptoed deftly from barmy left to subservient right in politics, remaining popular with both. Accepted Rhodri's Welsh Office job without a shudder of guilt. Choreographed the stitch-ups. Denounced Rhodri Morgan supporters as 'crypto-nationalist' and 'Trotskyists'. Has been compared with Odo, Star Trek's Shape-shifter who liquefies at the end of each day and sleeps in a bucket, then emerges later in any shape he wishes. Has the capacity of being on all sides - simultaneously. Prolific writer, permanently sun-tanned media junkie, specialising in non-attributable briefings, 'one of us' to Millbank, skilled television performer. Now Labour's Minister for Africa.

RATING: *Two flames: five pompoms.*

PAUL MURPHY

Obvious choice for the declining role of Secretary of State for Wales as act of gratitude for splendid job he did as Northern Ireland Minister. Incurably Blairist. Sybaritically fond of classical music and fine food, blissfully recalls using gold cutlery when guest of the French government, son of a miner loved being Minister-on-call in Hillsborough Castle, Third generation Irish, did not attend a Catholic secondary school and is thus a devout Catholic. Francophile. Possibly the only politician regularly accompanied by his spiritual adviser when on holiday. Has frontbench low level gravitas. Fierce opponent of devolution in 1979, now a reluctant convert. Passionate on curbing new powers to the Assembly, tribally Labour, good mimic (especially of Leo Abse), an absentee during the stitch-up. Oxford-educated historian, an enthusiastic cook and bachelor.

RATING: *One flame: one pompom.*

DON TOUHIG

Able former newspaper editor, ex-Councillor, came late into Commons. After fighting two nursery seats, secured hotly fought-over safe (?) Islwyn seat with support from the Kinnocks. Model New Labour gofer for Gordon Brown. Ambitious, pal since childhood of fellow catholic Paul Murphy, can be pompous. Seamstress-in-Chief of stitch-ups, won the Wales on Sunday 'Reef Knot Award for Intellectual Gymnastics'. Ministerial job chance now delayed as a result of his acting as conduit to 'leak' of information which forced apology to Commons and his resignation as PPS. Might resurrect political career through friendship with Paul Murphy.

RATING: *One flame (flickering): four pompoms.*

WAYNE DAVID

Able, youngish ex-MEP, former Leader of British Socialist Group of MEPs, won his niche in history by losing the Rhondda in the Assembly elections. Set to return to politics via retiring MP's seat (Aberavon or Rhondda?), now employed advising on Europe. Mentioned as a possible Assembly Leadership candidate, played small public role in the stitch-up. Alun supporter, affable, ambitious, has few enemies, unexciting, not renowned for originality, was at home among the Euro-drivel. An exception among MEPs, he used his Euro-gold for its intended purpose to employ staff. Close friend of Rhondda Labour godfather Ken Hopkins.

RATING: *One flame: two pompoms*

JOHN MAREK

MP and AM for Wrexham, Czech parents. Basketball player, international bridge player, former Health & Treasury Spokesman '85 - '92. A wow in Eastern Europe because he is fluent in Czech. Very large majority (37%) in Assembly elections, as did many other Rhodri supporting candidates. Led the North Wales battle against the Stitch-ups. Writes column for the Wrexham Leader. Has taken an independent line in Assembly debates. Was 'soft left', now fierce and persuasive critic of Blairism. Dangerously intelligent, criticised Labour's Assembly election campaign for 'concentrating the attack too much on Plaid Cymru'. Surprisingly not included in Alun Michael's Assembly Cabinet, was accused by Tory Assembly Leader Nick Bourne of being a Party on his own.

RATING: *Four flames.*

TERRY THOMAS

Gained a reputation as a formidable orator and NUM leader. Career move to GMB caused by disappearing miners. Godfather to Peter Hain's adoption in Neath. Malleable ideology, has come from critic of the Falklands war to pussy cat Blairist. Dominator of Labour's Welsh Executive for an eternity. Now retired, possible New Labour Lord, has (jokingly?) volunteered for post as Governor General of Bermuda. Enthusiastic stitch-up collaborator, still on the Welsh Executive, truculent, plotter.

RATING: *One flame: five pompoms.*

GEORGE WRIGHT

Recently retired, doyen of Welsh Trade Unionists for three decades. Probably learned the dirty tricks of electioneering because they were used against him when he twice lost ballots for the General Secretary of the TGWU. Time and political fashions have been unkind to him. Once seen as the Unions' voice of reason and moderation, is now judged to be an old fashioned fixer. Deferential to all authority, Blair/Callaghan loyalist, campaigned brilliantly for devolution in 1979 when he fell out with Neil Kinnock, the scar of defeat never healed. Possible candidate for ermine.

RATING: *Two flames: four pompoms*

ROGER WARREN EVANS

The Third Man in the Leadership Election. 63 year old financial manager, describes himself as 'socialist businessman'. Ex-Hackney Councillor, born in Gower where he now lives. Stood in Leadership election to 'avoid the Party crucifying itself by polarising choices between Rhodri and Alun', and to challenge monopoly of choice by MPs. Late arrival in the contest (Nov 15) and lack of Union support finished him off. Has written his own 'Little Red Book'. Leading campaigner for fair pensions, fully functioning brain, original, free thinker.

RATING: *Two flames.*

KEVIN MORGAN

Cerebral, impassioned, talented professor. Born-again devolutionist, strove to have a balanced Assembly candidate selection panel, including business interests. Knowledgeable about Welsh industry, particularly hi-tech. Attacked stitch-ups in choice of candidates within individual constituencies. Writing (with Geoff Mungham) a history of recent events in Welsh politics. Acerbic commentator on the stitch-up. Blair critic, Rhodri Morgan supporter, fearless, idealist.

RATING: *Three flames.*

GARETH HUGHES

Housing specialist, lifelong devotee of devolution, has challenged the Welsh Executive Establishment and paid the penalty of elimination from candidates' list. Impassioned on Welsh issues, has long sought Parliamentary seat, without success. Ex-Chair of Caerphilly constituency Labour Party and friend of Ron Davies. If a devolved / autonomous / independent Welsh Labour Party ever happens, Gareth will be its inspiration. Impassioned, latent energy of a coiled spring, broods.

RATING: *Three flames.*

NICK AINGER

Popular MP for Carmarthen after snatching Pembrokeshire seat from uncharismatic Tory. In the Alun-loop, but ultimately a victim of the stitch-up. Hitched his wagon to the stars of Ron Davies and Alun Michael as Parliamentary gofer. Now both have little Westminster influence. Superb reputation as hyperactive and resourceful constituency MP. Loyal and principled, worked as docker before Parliamentary career. Won gofer triple crown with appointment as PPS to Paul Murphy. Principled, humorous, lover of life and of dogs.

RATING: *Three flames: one pompom.*

DAVID HANSON

Good natured North Walian do-gooder, quietly risen to be new

Minister at the Welsh Office with few people having noticed that he is an MP. Has no enemies, even though he has been Welsh Whip. Rarely emotes, campaigned on glue sniffing deaths, spouse of Margaret who recently fought a Cheshire by-election. No detectable ideology, Labour by birth. In the Alun-loop, ambitious, one of the tricoteuses of the stitch-up, self-deprecating.

RATING: *Three pompoms.*

ANDREW DAVIES

Assembly Member (AM) for Swansea West. Rare survivor of many years working as Labour Party Wales apparatchik without suffering significant damage to his brain or soul. Defends the rules for selecting Assembly candidates that he devised, but not the final results. Rhodri and CYFLE (Campaign for democracy in Welsh Labour Executive) supporter. Now Business Manager in the Assembly, worked for lobbying firm when all else failed. Intelligent, honourable and subtle, a rarity in the world of politics. Sanguine.

RATING: *Two flames.*

KEVIN BRENNAN

Amiable ex-President of the Oxford Union, contemporary and friend of William Hague, Rhodri's researcher. Rare wit in Welsh politics and highly intelligent. Possible future AM or MP. From Torfaen (Paul Murphy groupie then, though he now denies it), Cardiff Councillor. As Rhodri's campaign manager, frequently outgunned Peter Hain and professional team in the Alun-loop. Going places politically, shrewd, creative.

RATING: *Four flames*

LLEW SMITH

MP for former Aneurin Bevan and Michael Foot seat of Blaenau Gwent, passionate believer in the Labour Party manifesto - of 1945. Thinks all subsequent changes are bad. Former MEP, avoided the Euro temptations. Was one of only six declared supporters of Rhodri in first election, then was Alun's most left-wing supporter in second election. Former winner of the Freedom of Information award. Occasionall escapes from his Keir Hardie Socialist time warp. Against: devolution nationalism; nuclear power; PFI. For: Blaenau Gwent; Nye Bevan; per manent revolution against Blairism.Early school leaver; self-educated ex-WEA teacher. earnest anachronism, bearded, predictable.

RATING: *One Flame: one pompom.*

KEN HOPKINS

Omnipresent fixer in Welsh Labour Circles, retired Director of Education, moved painlessly from 'Old Valleys Labourism' to 'New Labour', praised as 'best teacher in his school' by one Welsh M described AM Kirsty Williams and MEP Eluned Morgan as 'little girls assists AM as researcher, Welsh New Labour 'trustee' allowed to mak excruciatingly 'loyalist' on message speech at Bournemout Conference, calls the shots in Rhondda constituency which was lost Plaid Cymru in Assembly election, active behind the scenes in Alu campaign, establishment figure, retired, in his seventies, was a 'list' can didate, now reluctant devolutionist, possible candidate for ermine.

RATING: *Four pompoms*

LEIGHTON ANDREWS

A lobbyist recently metamorphosised into a 'consultant'. Heaped prais on Peter Hain booklet at the same time that Peter wrote a foreword t Leighton's book heaping praise on Leighton. Leighton said 'Pet believes in mutual support'. Given a place on a quango by Willia Hague in 1996. Leading role in referendum campaign, the victory which he attributes to a logo he picked. Hagiographer to Alun Michae frequently seen around the Assembly building. Oleaginous, accommc dating, feline, apprentice shape-shifter.

RATING: *Four pompoms.*

THE AUTHOR

A blend of poet and peasant, saint and sinner; appearance of aging hipp inspires loathing and love in roughly equal measures. Named by Ron Davies as the 'conscience of the Labour Party' and by another Welsh MP as 'an embittered has-been'. Permanent back-bencher by choice, a decision warmly supported by Tony Blair. For: Sam and family and domestic menagerie (frequently has kittens and pups to home); hi-tech; devolution; decent pensions; quality politics. Against: financial rip-offs; sleaze; drug prohibition; stitch-ups; lobbyists and other deceivers., writing a book on 'The Art of Coarse Politics.'

RATING: ?

WALES EXECUTIVE

Execrable. An expensive organism that lacks any useful function apart from organising Welsh Night (a raffle, a sing-song and a booze-up) at Conference. This year's event was Folleted by Jessica Morden. Must be reformed (by CYFLE?), genetically transformed, or humanely destroyed.

RATING: *Five pompoms.*

QUOTES

'Does a one-legged duck swim in circles?' Rhodri Morgan, in answer to the Paxman question, 'Will you stand for Leader?'

'Rhodri is a long-standing friend of mine and I have publicly said how much I admire him' Peter Hain.

'There will be no fixes, no attempt to deny anybody their rights' Peter Hain.

'Alun is London's choice, New Labour: Rhodri is Wales ' choice, True Labour' Welsh MP.

'This nonsense must stop' Don Touhig on non-existent faxes.

'The Morgan camp are damaging the Labour Party with anonymous briefings and faxes, lies and wild allegations' Peter Hain.

'Peter Hain has no time for the fixers of Old Labour' Leighton Andrews.

'My Grandmother was a Seamstress in Llanrhaedr-ym-Mochnant' Alun Michael justifying list seat, not stitch up.

'My nation calls' Wayne David on why he stood down as an MEP.

'Rhodri is the natural Leader of Wales' Tyrone O'Sullivan.

'God, how I wish he was' – George Wright when asked if he would like Ron Davies as Assembly Leader.

'In New Labour, MP stands for Material for Promotion, Mandelson Poodle and Millbank Pagee' – Rhodri Morgan.

'There are lots of Trotskyists in UNISON out to damage the Labour Party' – Peter Hain.

'Sleaze-free politics, real democracy, truly open government, the people's prioritie – these are the themes that will run through my campaign' – Rhodri Morgan.

'Nobody does it better' Hagiographer Leighton Andrews on Alun Michael.

'There is a schizophrenic at the centre of New Labour and his name is Tony Blair' Observer columnist Andrew Rawnsley .

'I put my seal on Alun Michael the day I appointed him Secretary of State Tony Blair.

'I wasn't a jersey-warmer for Ron Davies, and I'm not one for Alun Michae Rhodri Morgan.

'The lobsters of Wales should escape from their pots' Alun Michael.

'The Labour Party emerged out of the bowels of the Trade Union movemen Ernest Bevin.

'Why don't you tell him to piss off?' Mo Mowlam when Alun's aide threa ened a hack.

'It is a race between the clever scholar and the classroom swot. One has wit, originality and enthusiasm, the other works hard to get things done. Morgan has the air of a mad professor; Michael is like the snooker ace Steve Davies - boringly reliable' Guardian journalist Andy MacSmith.

'Alun Morgan (sic) has equal qualities, he's the Secretary of State' George Wright.

'Tony Blair was the best boss I've ever had' Rhodri Morgan.

'I was perfectly prepared to believe that Alun is the Prime Minister's choice to lead the Welsh Assembly because he regularly plumps up the cushions on his sofa' Roy Hattersley.

'It goes back to Ancient Greece, it's called democracy. It has reached Wales, but only in patches' Rhodri Morgan.

'This is the start of something where we need to work together to get the problem done (sic)' Tony Blair.

'Cynulliad y werin, nid Cynulliad y crachach' 'An Assembly of the people, not an Assembly of the establishment' Rhodri Morgan.

'I give you my personal guarantee that under my leadership the Assembly will be free of sleaze, free of patronage, and free of machine politics' Rhodri Morgan.

'Forced twinning of Welsh constituencies was as popular as Saddam Hussein's attempt to twin Iraq with Kuwait was - in Kuwait' Rhodri Morgan.

'Nobody's ever heard of Alun Michael here. Rhodri Morgan's one of us. My favourite was Maggie Thatcher' Cardiff Taxi driver.

'Labour has an EXITing strategy for pensioners' centrally produced Labour leaflet.

'If Labour lost the Rhondda it would be a political earthquake that would bus the seismograph' Matthew Engel.

'To go down a separatist road would be suicide for us politically' Don Touhig MP for Plaid-gained Islwyn.

'If the results turn out as we predict, then observers would have to acknowledg that this is a major triumph for the Labour Party' Peter Hain, 7th May 1999 am.

'Tony, I've lost the Rhondda, Islwyn and Llanelli' Peter Hain, 7th May 1999 pm (apocryphal).

'So, you're losing out of the goodness of your own hearts, then, are you?' BBC presenter Betsan Powys to Peter Hain.

'In the election of the Secretary of State for Wales last Saturday, the Labour Part conducted itself fairly' Ray Powell MP.

'It was a pantomime of democracy. Labour seems not to know the damage it ha done to the principle of devolution' Kevin Morgan.

'Rehabilitation is a process, not an event' Anon on Ron Davies, May 99

'Lionel Jospin's socialism is popular in Wales: in LLanelli they sing 'Josp Fach' Rhodri Morgan.

THE PRECEPTS OF POMPOM-ISM

1
Truth is the opinion of the majority and changes daily.

2
A promise is infinitely malleable.

3
Power pumps the lifeblood of Pompom-ism.

4
Rights are the servants of expediency.

5
Knowledge, intelligence and originality are diversions from the truth.

6
Election results are decided by leaders, not electorates.

7
Everything can be bought, including loyalty and faith.

8
A pledge is for elections, not a for a full term.

9
Love of democracy is the enemy of efficiency.

10
Select the desired outcome and adjust your principles to achieve it.

11

Election cheating is no gamble: history is written by winners.

12

The wages of sin are bounteous and often paid in ermine.

13

The loyalty that is most admirable is loyalty to superiors.

14

Between error and truth, chaos and order, sin and virtue lies
the third way.

15

Only the future is certain: the past is always changing.

Countdown

Sep. 19th 1998	Ron Davies beats Rhodri Morgan as Leader in waiting.
Oct. 26th 1998	Ron Davies incident on Clapham Common.
Oct. 27th 1998	Ron Davies resigns as SOS. Replaced by Alun Michael.
Sep. 30th 1998	Ron Davies resigns as Leader.
Nov. 5th 1998	Alun announces he will run for Leader.
Nov. 9th 1998	Electoral timetable and college approved.
Nov. 27th 1998	Blair's first visit to Wales to back Alun.
Dec. 21st 1998	Alun abandons Constituency option, goes for list seat.
Jan.14th 1999	Downing Street Reception.
Jan.15th 1999	Blair's second campaigning visit to Wales.
Jan.16th 1999	AEEU back Alun without Omov.
Jan. 22nd 1999	TGWU back Alun without Omov.
Feb.1st 1999	Major telephone poll gives Rhodri 90% support.
Feb.2nd 1999	Blair's third visit to Wales.
Feb.6th 1999	Rhodri wins Omov of UNISON by 3 to 1.
Feb.11th 1999	Michael given top spot in hotly disputed candidates' lists.
Feb.19th 1999	GMB back Alun without Omov.
Feb.20th 1999	Alun is declared winner.
May. 6th 1999	Assembly Elections.
July 17th 1999	First meeting of CYFLE to rebuild democracy

Worse than dead

'If everything on earth were rational, nothing would happen'
Dostoevsky.

A WEEK BEFORE the night of the walk on Clapham Common, I was phoned by Ron Davies's Parliamentary Private Secretary, Nick Ainger. Ron was driving up to London from Wales and would like us to join him for a meal.

Great. There was no whip in the Commons so we were free to leave Westminster and dine out in a favourite Thai restaurant at Lavender Hill. It is within walking distance of the Battersea house that Ron has shared with three other MPs for 15 years. Any chance of escaping the claustrophobic world of Parliament was welcome and we rarely missed the pleasure of eating out in the evenings. It happened about once a fortnight. Usually there were five or six of us eating. Ron's adviser Huw Roberts and Welsh Officer Minister Jon Owen Jones were regulars. Peter Hain put in the occasional appearance.

Ron told us how much he now enjoyed driving up to London alone. He was entitled to use his chauffeured Ministerial car. It was bliss at first, but the novelty had now staled. He missed listening to his favourite music and his taped Welsh lessons. It was a great evening. This was a new relaxed Ron. His life had been a constant strain since he took office eighteen months earlier.

Immediately after a gruelling General Election he had been pitch-forked into unremitting work. The Welsh Assembly legislation had to be bludgeoned through a disagreeable, obstinate Parliament. The referendum campaign had been an exhausting, nerve-jangling anguish. Even after that, there was no respite.

The strain continued with a bruising contest with Rhodri Morgan for Leadership of the Party in Wales. Simultaneously, he had to perform the role of Secretary of State. He had been opposed on all sides. He was constantly patronised by New Labour and sneered at by some Old Labour Welsh veterans. Understandably, he was often frazzled and tense.

Months later, he vividly described that period:

Before I resigned I almost ceased to exist as a person. I was Secretary of State and the pressure was on my time from first thing in the morning to last thing at night. I enjoyed it enormously, but every conversation you have is about defending government policy or listening to what people have to say or explaining what you are going to do next. Never a conversation about bird watching or Llanelli versus Cardiff the previous week or the latest film.

For all of us, the meals out were welcome interruptions of life on duty. There were just three of us at the Thai restaurant that night. The chat was about the Opening Day of the Assembly. A repeat of the march of children organised by Urdd Gobaith Cymru (The Welsh Youth Organisation) to celebrate their anniversary was favoured. Ron was keen. His daughter had taken part in the original procession earlier that year.

The alternative was a military display that no politicians wanted. This was favoured by the royal lick spittles. The royal involvement was being pressed as part of their public relations campaign to re-invent royalty. The excitement at the coming event was palpable. Ron's place in Welsh history was now secure. His persistent, tireless work had won Wales its Assembly.

The most wounding lesson in Welsh history is the treachery of some of our past leaders. Over the last 150 years, a succession of politicians left Wales for London with the promise of 'home rule' on their lips. Seduced by Westminster and the trappings of power, none had delivered. Now, for the first time since the fifteenth century, we were about to have our own ruling body on the soil of our own country. Llywelyn ein Llyw Olaf, Owen Glyndwr, Robert Owen, Emrys ap Iwan, Aneurin Bevan and, now, Ron Davies. It was an agreeable thought.

Not once did I suspect that Ron had a life in London that was unknown to those of us who believed that we were his closest friends. That night, we were happy that the obstacles of winning the election, the referendum and the Leadership vote were behind us. Now it was downhill all the way to the Assembly with a certain Labour Party majority. We thought.... Tony Blair is in Downing Street, Ron is in the

Welsh Office, the Welsh Nation was about to be reborn. All was right with the world.

The awful coming events cast no shadows before them. We had no inkling that the sky was about to fall in on all of us. No sign that the Party was on the edge of twelve months of the most bitter conflict in our history.

Exactly a week later, Welsh Whip David Hanson received a call from Ron on his pager. The call was timed at 7.15 pm. There were two 3-line votes that evening. The first was at 7.00 pm and the second at 10.00 pm. Ron had not arranged to be absent. Had he asked, he would certainly have been excused because of his Ministerial duties. He had planned to be in the Commons that evening. Something unexpected had happened. The message apologised for Ron's absence from the 7.00 pm vote, and said that he was in London, but would probably miss the 10.00 pm vote too.

This reinforces the view of his closest friends that his behaviour that night was not planned but the result of sudden impulse. One close friend argues that this was the first time that Ron had ever, in the words of Kevin Morgan, 'taken a walk on the wildside' in London. The friend worked closely with him and would have been aware of any previous unexplained absences. The diaries of Secretaries of State are planned well in advance, without gaps for spontaneous peregrinations.

There was no cold Autumn rain where I was that night. Family illness had delayed our holiday. We were in Israel when the thunderbolt struck. My wife Sam explained. 'It's just been announced on Sky that Alun Michael has been appointed Secretary of State for Wales'.

The surroundings in which I heard the shattering news were as exotic and incongruous as the news itself. I was sipping beer in a Tel Aviv Hotel, watching a group of Hungarian folk dancers. My jaw dropped in disbelief. The message was incomprehensible. Sam tried again. 'Sky said Alun's got the job following the demise of Ron Davies'. 'He's dead? ... ', I spluttered.

'No, It's probably worse than that', Sam replied. I snorted at the front page of the Sun shown on Sky. It mentioned 'gay sex'. Ron, gay? This is a man I had known as a close and trusted friend for 20 years. Heterosexual sex, possibly. But not homosexual. Along with many of Ron's closest friends, I had never heard a whisper of any scandal on these lines.

The only nagging doubt was a remark he made to Rhodri in August 1998 during their election fight. 'It doesn't matter very much. I don't expect to be in politics much longer'. It was puzzling and was put down to a passing moment of desolation. The closer his friends were to him the less we knew him. Ron did have a roving eye after a few beers. He became verbally predatory to women. That is no different to many other middle aged 'mouth and trousers' males. This was Ron the 'valley boy' acting out his role. Nevertheless, even in the fetid hothouse of the Commons, where tales of testosterone overload are common, I never heard any serious accusations Ron was playing away from home.

It was hard to take in. Ron Davies, my friend, was now an item of prurient international news. I watched him on Sky. He seemed confident and clear. His rugged features looked more composed than usual. His ruddy complexion was toned down. For once, his face did not looked as though it had been trampled on by a rugby scrum. Had he used the make-up he normally spurned? He explained that it was a 'moment of madness'. He had been mugged ... so he had resigned. The story made no sense.

I rang Nick Ainger the next day from a hotel overlooking the Sea of Galilee. 'What the hell's going on?' I asked. 'Dunno', said the ever loyal Nick. 'Would Ron like a chat? Shall I ring him?' I offered. 'No point' said Nick, 'he's not talking to anyone'. Nick had sacrificed his own political ambitions to serve Ron in the thankless gofer role of Parliamentary Private Secretary. If Ron's career was collapsing, so was Nick's. It was grotesquely unfair. Nick deserved an explanation. We could not fathom it out. Nick and I swapped incredulities about any possibility that Ron was gay. No-one had ever told us.

Nick said that Alun Michael, Ron's successor, had offered him the job of PPS. 'Take it' I said, in the belief that it would be best for Nick. The advice was superfluous: Nick already had. 'Alun would like to see you next Thursday. Nine o' clock in the Welsh Office', Nick said, already carrying out his role as go-between between Minister and backbencher. Perhaps Alun would know what was going on. I was looking forward to an explanation, something that would make sense of this lunacy .

When I returned home, I trawled through the back copies of newspapers that had stacked up. I studied every word of Ron's account of the escapade. It came across as 'Ron was out strolling on Clapham Common. He met a Rastafarian stranger. They chatted. Ron, the

Secretary of State for Wales, found much to talk about with the Rasta. His occupation appeared to be acquiring boys and women for clients. Ron and the Rasta had so much in common, they decided to have a meal. They then spent the next two hours together'. Huh?

I empathised with the Western Mail 's news and comment.

It is indeed bizarre that the then Welsh Secretary next drove along to a block of flats in south London to pick up two more strangers and ended up on a Brixton housing estate known as 'crack alley', having been invited' for a meal.

Mr Davies said there was no sex or drugs link. He was simply the victim of a terrible crime. But resigning as a Cabinet Minister for this is surely nonsensical. Is it, as one wit suggested, that Labour is now 'tough on crime and tough on the victims of crime'? To some, it just does not stack up.

Very sadly, it never did stack up. Ron fought a vigorous battle to re-establish his reputation. Being more open and frank about his 'moment of madness' might have helped. He bitterly regretted using that phrase which was suggested to him by Alastair Campbell. It was never plausible to describe the protracted events as a single moment of madness. His strategy did not work in time to restore his credibility as future Leader of the Welsh Assembly. The accepted wisdom in announcing bad news is: 'Tell it soon; Tell it all; Tell it truthfully'. Ron did not get any further than telling it soon.

The perceptive Kevin Morgan observed:

> *Ron Davies' walk on the wildside may prove to be one of the defining moments of modern Welsh politics. He was the cement that held together the control needs of New Labour in London and the Party Bosses in Wales with the aspirations of many Labour members here for more say over their own Party, and the desire of many people for a new politics. Now he has gone the struggle between those asking for more democracy and those seeking to secure their own political future is out in the open. The outcome of this struggle will decide the fate of the Assembly and New Wales.*

Even though the focus was still on Ron, the Wales on Sunday newspaper, with admirable prescience, said on November 1st 'If Messrs Michael and Morgan contested an election, the result would probably depend on whether the Unions allow their rank and file members to participate in the ballot'. After initially claiming that he still hoped to lead the Assembly, pressure from the press forced him to withdraw as the aspirant Leader. Ron, the author of devolution, could no longer direct its genesis.

The settled Welsh political landscape heaved and became unrecognisable.

SERENITY RAVAGED

'Everything is for sale, even friendship'
Ferengi Rule of Acquisition No 121.

ON THE MORNING after Ron's walk, Tuesday October 27th, Alun Michael's life was one of sweet, frantic serenity. He inhabited the world which he had created around himself. It is the place where he loves to live. He was dining at Christopher's at lunchtime. Nothing warned him that he was at the gates of hell.

Alun was a happy man, with good reason. He had achieved everything he had ever wanted from life. His marriage was mature and fulfilled. His beloved wife Mary was with him in his comfortable new London flat. His five children were now grown up and living the lives they had chosen. The job he loved was acting as a catalyst to reform of the voluntary structure. He had built a network of respectful contacts in the empire of Home Office work. His years as a shadow Minister with Tony Blair in opposition had earned him respect and gratitude. Jack Straw found him an ideal, amiable helper who would never stand in his light.

Christopher's is off the Strand, in rooms below what used to be a brothel. It has an Italianate style. The operatic background music appeals to Alun, a veteran friend of the Welsh National Opera. Reuben Waller, the maitre d'hote, conveyed the message to Alun that 10 Downing Street wanted him to call. Alun left immediately. He had not touched the lunch he had ordered.

It has yet to be revealed what happened between Blair and Michael. Alun was interviewed on the steps of the Welsh Office. He refused to be drawn on Ron's demise except to express regret. Inside the Welsh Office, he announced that the only decision he was going to take that day was whether he was going to have milk in his coffee.

It was Wednesday when I returned from Israel. The 'Welsh Table' at the Commons was buzzing. Traditionally, it was the gathering point for Welsh members, in the spot where a picture of Lloyd George used to hang. Alun made a bee-line for me and sat on the opposite side of the table. I congratulated him briefly. Without any preliminaries he said with emphasis: 'You know, more than anyone, that I have campaigned for devolution, in the seventies and before that ... Now will you support me for Leader?'

I confirmed that he had worked for devolution in 1979 but I firmly told him that I would not support him as Leader. His face changed to the 'smacked bum' look I knew so well. 'Anyway, I'm seeing you tomorrow, we'll talk about it then'.

When we met at Gwydyr House, I begged him not to stand as Leader. Alun had been a pal since I first met him in 1971. He was the education correspondent of the South Wales Echo. I was campaigning to open a Welsh language school in Newport. His children attended Welsh language school in Cardiff. We were allies in that and in many other battles over the next 30 years.

Alun, Rhodri, Paul Murphy and I shared our first office in Parliament when we were all first elected in 1987. For eleven years Alun and I also shared a flat and a mortgage at the Elephant and Castle. I have always liked and admired him. As an old friend, I had been pleased that he had his dream job at the Home Office. Secretary of State for Wales was a move for the worse, not the better.

Although it was a Cabinet position, it could not be an improvement on the perfection of his Home Office job. I renewed my good wishes but pleaded with him to change his mind on the Leadership of the Welsh Assembly.

I repeated the accepted wisdom that his recognised enthusiasm in 1979 had not been apparent in the '97 referendum. That accusation had been widely made. But it wounded him. Again he denied that he had lost interest and claimed that he did his bit in '97 as well as in '79. He mentioned his visit to Splott Market.

'Yes', I said, 'but that was the day when Donald Dewar came to your constituency. You had no choice. I am pretty certain that I spent more time campaigning in Cardiff than you did this time.' He did not press the point. He asked me to back his campaign. I argued that there should be no campaign.

You've got enough on your plate learning this job and setting up the Assembly'. The elected members of the Welsh Assembly will chose their leader after the election in May. Why divide the Party when the elected Assembly Members may overturn the decision anyway?

This time, I argued, Rhodri should lead the campaign. He would do it brilliantly and win Labour a majority in the Assembly. Alun could do the business as Secretary of State. The choice of First Secretary of the Assembly could be made in a single vote after the election. Surely this would be a sensible, peaceful, practical solution, one that would heal wounds, not deepen them?

The alternative was an inevitably bitter, divisive campaign that would damage Alun and throw the Party into turmoil. I believed that Alun would lose any fair vote. Tony Blair had the unchallenged right to appoint Alun to his Cabinet. But he had no right to appoint the Labour Leader in the Assembly. That is the job of the members of the Labour Party in Wales. 'It's a process called devolution', I helpfully reminded him.

There was no meeting of minds. The impression I had was that Downing Street had decided that Alun should force an election. Not for the first, or last, time, the neurotic need of Downing Street to control everything was poisoning the harmony of the Labour Party.

In the naive belief that the election was going to be a fair measure of opinion in the Welsh Party, I guaranteed to him that he would lose. 'You don't understand how angry the Party is now'. He angrily asked where I thought he had been for the last few months, 'I know what's going on in the Party' he snapped.

Gently, I suggested that the view of Wales from the Home Office was not as clear as it was from the backbenches. I reminded him of the wound of the sacking of Win Griffiths.

As an 'off message' Labour MP, I am not in the habit of lavishing praise on Ministers. But, in an unguarded, sudden display of sincerity in the Welsh Grand Committee's meeting in Merthyr in June 1998, I had publicly thanked Win Griffiths for the high quality of his work.

In his twenty years in Welsh politics, Win has won universal respect as a decent, honourable, hard-working politician. He openly confessed that he had two skeletons in his cupboard. He was born in South Africa and he was named after Winston Churchill. As a Welsh Office Minister, his 60 hour a week work-schedule and his attention to detail won admiration from everybody, including Tony Blair.

Two weeks after I had praised him, he was sacked. Why? Detective work by journalists and others has revealed the true, unpleasant story. The Observer had forecast that Win would be dropped a few days before it happened. The well had been poisoned.

Without the consent or cooperation of any MP elected by the people of Wales, he was to lose his job. Win was interviewed by Blair on Monday and dismissed.

The problem was that Win did not have friends and patrons in high places. As a teetotaller, he rightly steers clear of much of the boozy round of Commons social events. Pressure had been on to give a Ministerial job to other pushy MPs who had friends in Cabinet. A vacancy had to be created. Win's job was sacrificed.

Happily, the plan mis-fired. The one who put the knife in did not get the job. The furious reaction from Welsh MPs against the sacking of Win hit the national media early in the week. I toured every broadcasting studio who would have me and denounced the sacking. All the other sacrificial lambs of sacked Ministers had gone without a bleat. Win gave interviews saying he did not know what he had done wrong.

Did Win's planned replacement have friends in high places? He did. The row embarrassed the spin doctors who returned to their drawing boards.

At 4.15 pm on the Tuesday of that week, a very strange event occurred. Although Win's departure had been planned since Sunday there was no name for his successor on the list of new Ministers circulated to a press Conference by spin supremo Alastair Campbell. A Welsh hack asked why.

Alastair gave the baffling reply, 'Because we are trying to snub Paul Flynn'. The humour of this joke is beyond me. What it did reveal was that there had been a change of plan.

Ron Davies had been excluded from the decision to sack Win, but he insisted on having his say on the replacement. Cardiff Central MP Jon Owen Jones had no part in the undermining of Win but had long served in the thankless job of Welsh whip.

Jon had deferred his chance of Ministerial office in 1997 in order to stay as whip and steer the devolution bill through Parliament. Some thought he had forfeited permanently his Ministerial hopes.

A sad story had a happy ending. Jon achieved office on the same day that Parliament gave Wales more self-government than we have had for five centuries. I was beginning to warm to Alastair. Appointing one of my closest friends to a job he loved was the nicest 'snub' I have ever had.

The Welsh Group of Labour MPs were upset at our meeting on Tuesday of that week. We voted to tell Tony about it. Secretary Don Touhig wrote to Tony. So did I as Chair. My letter was uninfluenced by any Ministerial ambitions. Even better, I had the rare good luck to be called by Speaker Betty Boothroyd at Prime Minister's Question Time the following day:

Mr. Paul Flynn (Newport, West): *Has the Prime Minister seen the tributes paid this morning to my hon. Friend the Member for Bridgend (Mr. Griffiths), saying that he has served his country and his Party remarkably well as a Welsh Office Minister? Is he aware that the Welsh group of Labour Members is bewildered and unhappy about the decision to sack him? What is the Prime Minister's assessment of the value of my hon. Friend's work as a Welsh Office Minister?*

The Prime Minister: *Of course I value the work that my hon. Friend the Member for Bridgend (Mr. Griffiths) has done. I understand the fact that when people leave the government, for whatever reason, they may feel concerned about it, but I, as Prime Minister, have to decide who should serve in the government, and in what position. That has always been the case with Prime Ministers, and it will continue to be the case with me.*

So, Tony knows best. The views of Welsh MPs count for nothing. Win's sacking was a humiliating blow to the Party. A month later there was another kicking for the Party in Wales. There was bitter resentment at the 'fixing' of the selection of Euro candidates. I tried another tack with Alun. Will this be another poke in the eye for the Party members in Wales? Lyndon Harrison all over again?

In late September 1998, the Welsh Labour Party delegates to National Conference shared a rare moment of unanimity. The Labour leadership was accused of 'parachuting in' a right-wing, English, Blairite politician as one of its top three candidates for Wales in the European

Parliamentary elections.

There was fury that the candidates were picked by a central panel rather than constituency votes or a one-member-one-vote (Omov) ballot of all Welsh members. Under the new PR system, Labour was tipped to get three of the five seats. The top three places were likely to get to Strasbourg. There was no chance for the fourth and fifth choices. They were the sitting Welsh MEPs Joe Wilson and Dave Morris.

Only two delegates from Wales had a tiny voice in the selection which picked Euro MPs Glenys Kinnock and Eluned Morgan. They were placed in the first and second positions respectively. But it was the choice of Cheshire MEP Lyndon Harrison in third place that enraged the Party. He had failed to be nominated for his own area. This looked terminal for the careers of the two Welsh male MPs.

Llew Smith, ex-MEP and MP for Blaenau Gwent, said: 'They are parachuting in New Labour people. It's nothing to do with democracy but it's about destroying one wing of the Party and that's the left.' Later, Llew revised his ideas. He learned that in some instances it was good to love parachuting and good to disapprove of Omov.

A Labour Party spokeswoman proved how far the Welsh Party had departed from reality and said the system used to select the Euro list was 'democratic'. As for imposing a candidate from England, she said, 'They were all chosen on their merits. They were all asked the same questions'.

David Morris later objected strongly to the way that he was questioned, especially on his time as Chair of CND Wales. The Party reeled. It was the delegates at National Conference who expressed the united anger of Party members. Ron was asked to accompany the delegates to a meeting with Party officials. Blair had sent him a message to 'sort it out'. Ron felt he was being expected to defended a decision he could not support and in which he had no role against a wave of hostility from the Party in Wales.

A nod and a wink was given that something would be done. But no-one knew how they could persuade Lyndon to abandon his political career and the financial and 'bon viveur' consolations of Europe.

This was my final clincher of an argument with Alun in the Welsh Office. He would be seen as another Lyndon Harrison, being parachuted into Wales. Alun stared back. I could have been talking in Polish for all my words meant to him. His eyes were focussed on a painting of a cellist hanging over the fireplace of his Gwydyr House office. Perhaps he seeing in the blue folds of her dress an apparition of Tony Blair.

His mind had been made up for him. The decision and the dangerous strategy was set in permafrost by Tony Blair. Later that day, he announced he had decided to stand for election as aspirant First Secretary of Wales 'after consulting his close friends'.

I wonder who they were.

POODLE OR DRAGON?

'And still they gaz'd, and still the wonder grew, That one small head could carry all he knew'

Goldsmith.

FANTASY POLITICS then took over.

Alun's announcement was welcomed with wild cheering from a group of pressganged Millbank groupies. Never before or since has Alun stirred rapture from an audience. But it was not spontaneous. This was New Labour adulation, rehearsed and bogus. Later, in dire circumstances, Alun's groupies were asked to fake it again. Rumour has it that they practised with a video of the 65 standing ovations Ceaucescu received from his followers a few weeks before he was driven from power.

Rhodri's followers raised impromptu cheers, probably from his mates in the Strangers bar in the Commons. He was not into a Millbank manicured media announcement. Rhodri was the acclaimed choice of Party members. His rapport with live audiences had been proved by the surprisingly high vote he had achieved when challenging Ron Davies for the job. Dr Alan Williams MP said 'Rhodri fought Ron a good contest in September and took second place', hardly a major triumph for Rhodri as there were only two candidates.

Freshly sharpened knives were out from the Blair armoury. Rhodri's campaign had to be destroyed. The spinners were busy at their black craft. Dripped into the ears of the lobby hacks was the story that Blair had 'sacked' Rhodri from the Frontbench and replaced him with Peter Hain because he had an 'unsafe' pair of hands. He was 'erratic, unpredictable, a loose cannon'. Even worse, his house was 'untidy'.

Unpredictability and untidiness are traits that threaten the orderly

Utopia of New Labour. They twitched and fidgeted at the prospect of a Welsh Leader whose brain impulses could not be pre-determined into orderly submission. Downing Street certainly did not want someone who could not be trusted to fold and 'stack tidy' his back copies of the Western Mail.

Names other than Alun's were thrown into the pot. Fantasists in Downing Street suggested Neil or Glenys Kinnock as the very models of New Labour on-message correctness. Possible Leaders in waiting? It was reported that they were not interested. The irony would have been delicious if the prime saboteurs of devolution in 1979 became the beneficiaries in 1999. They were quickly forgotten because they could not be dis-entangled from their Euro-roles.

Even retiring MEP Wayne David had his supporters. They kept alive a forlorn hope that he could be the compromise choice. Having few opinions, he had few enemies. No-one foresaw that he was hurtling towards his personal political Armageddon.

Reality emerged and it became a two species race. A cartoon in the Times showed Blair throwing a coloured ebullient Red Dragon flag to the ground and replacing it with a downcast black and white sheep. Blair was saying 'Now that's the kind of Assembly Leader I want.' Another drew Alun as a fetching poodle.

The images were truthful and irresistible. All that both candidates did for the next three months reinforced the image of the Dragon versus the Poodle / Sheep.

A Wales on Sunday editorial was first to make the points that were to become the campaigns' mantras:

Rhodri is the only contender. He is wholeheartedly committed to Wales and passionately desires the role. Alun Michael has been hell-bent on carving a career for himself in Westminster. We don't want Blair's choice of a compromise candidate. Wales' very first First Secretary has to be more than a puppet.

The opening shots of the fight were fired at two public meetings held in early November. Coincidence had pre-arranged for Alun to be speaking at a Co-op Party love-in at Cardiff the same night that Rhodri addressed a Chartist Rally in Newport.

Alun said:

There is a self-destructive element in our psyche in Wales. A larger

42

country may be able to afford such luxuries, but we are small and vulnerable. We cannot afford such pettiness of spirit when we are a small nation with a fragile economy, immense social problems and a fractured identity.

Rhodri said:

For democracy to flourish in Wales people must realise what the Chartists knew: that without democracy and accountability the needs of ordinary working people will be ignored. Whoever leads us in the Assembly must be chosen democratically here in Wales.

The next morning, I was sparring on Radio Four's Today programme with one of Labour's old war horses, George Wright, the Gauleiter of the TGWU in Wales. In his Union, Wales is romantically identified as 'Region number four'.

George was a few months away from retirement. His career had been disappointing. There was one highlight over which he repeatedly reminisces. Out of the blue one day, Jim Callaghan, who was then Prime Minister, called at George's Caerphilly home. To George, these were the 'great days', when statesmen courted Trade Unionists.

George was the doyen of Welsh Trade Union leaders at a time when talent was thinly spread. He had been twice defeated in elections for the still powerful post of General Secretary of the TGWU. His career had included a leading role in the pro-devolution campaign of 1979. George judged himself to be the power broker. He plumped for Alun.

To John Humphries on the Today programme, I argued that 'a divisive election for the Leader of the Labour Group in the Welsh Assembly could be avoided if Rhodri was acknowledged as the choice of the people of Wales'.

Already, two opinion polls of Party members and potential candidates had shown Rhodri to have a massive lead. It would be preposterous to choose Alun who would be a Leader without credit facing a possible vote of no confidence at the first meeting of Assembly Members.

I recalled the meeting in Newport the previous evening attended by 200 Party members and supporters, two MPs and an MEP. No one supported the automatic choice of Alun. One of the MPs and the MEP may later have expressed a different opinion. But that night, everyone had backed a one member, one vote election.

George claimed that the TGWU could not afford an Omov ballot. Humphries helpfully branded George as an 'old fashioned Trade Union leader'. It gave me the chance of putting the boot into George as an old fixer arranging deals in now 'smoke-free rooms'. I said that Rhodri had been denied promotion because he did not fit the New Labour Party mould. He was judged to be 'too colourful, too lively, and too Welsh'.

Things became heated. At one point, I said Tony Benn when I meant Tony Blair. But I got my planned soundbite in: that 'Alun is London's choice, New Labour: Rhodri is Wales's choice, True Labour'. Obligingly, Anna Ford repeated it. 'It used to be Classic Labour. Now it's True Labour'.

The Today Programme is to Labour MPs and Millbank staff what matins are for monks. Attendance is obligatory, because the message determines the subject for contemplation for the day.

Margaret McDonagh, the about-to-be General Secretary of the Labour Party, was dutifully listening. She sought me out in the Commons a few days later. She harangued me with the news that Millbank were not interfering in the campaign. She told me to pass that message on to the Party in Wales. Tony Blair also complained later about criticism of his 'young team' at Millbank. Such sensitive creatures.

In the collective mind of the national media the image of the contest was beginning to form. The spin from Rhodri's team was being universally accepted by the national press. It fitted comfortably with the hacks' accurately cynical view of politics. Alun was being parachuted into Wales. Alun was Blair's poodle or sheep. Rhodri was the Welsh-bred dragon.

For perhaps the first time the Downing Street spinners had been out-spun. Almost all UK national papers carried cartoons depicting the dragon and the parachuted sheep or the poodle. The image became an indelible one.

'Surrender, While You're Ahead'

> *'Yet from those flames no Light,*
> *But rather darkness visible'*
>
> Milton.

Downing Street, we have a problem' was the message from New Labour Mission Control at Millbank.

Alun was facing certain defeat, even humiliation. This would be a novel experience for Alun, New Labour and Tony Blair. The polls and the soundings of the Party in Wales were unanimous. Rhodri was miles ahead of Alun.

The fate of the contest was likely to be determined by the method of the election. There was little dispute about the Ron Davies and Rhodri contest, the result of which had been entirely predictable. The Party had wanted an election that was, above all, quick. This time they were faced with the prospect of a result that Downing Street did not want. Stitch-ups had to be devised that would guarantee the election of the candidate who was not wanted by the electorate. The choice of system was up to the Labour Party Executive in Wales. Precept six of Pompomism had to be followed: 'Election results are decided by leaders, not electorates'.

The Labour Party Executive in Wales has rarely been a model of elevated debate and sophisticated democracy. Meetings jar and shudder with macho posturing and confrontational rows. Usually it was about nothing ideological or principled. Just a few truculent individuals out to get their way.

It was often decision making by shouting and bullying. In a meeting at Mold in 1997, a Council leader and a Trade Union boss had a nose to nose shouting match. It left a permanent scar on the memories of all those who endured the excruciating spectacle. 'Unbearable' was the kindest thing said about the event. The row was about ... what? Who knows? They have probably both forgotten now.

The towering rows interrupted the normal tedium of Welsh Labour decision making. That was through endless hours of tiresome low key bickering. The outcome was of secondary importance. It's the rucking and fighting that matter. A definition of the deprived person in Wales is someone who is not on any committee. The Welsh Executive is a Big Committee, and membership is a bruising but prized antidote to deprivation.

In 1998-99, the Executive majority became a pliant, mindless servant of Blairism. It combined the worst of Old Labour bullying with abject New Labour vote-rigging. Without a blush, a prominent, ennobled Welsh Trade Union figure said in July that he always did what the Labour Party told him to do. He probably sees that as principled in its own way, presuming, of course, that one first accepts the doctrine of the infallibility of Blairism. He and many others were later to discover the force of the 12th Precept of Pompomism: 'The wages of sin are bounteous and sometimes paid in ermine'.

The Executive was then made up of three sections. A third were constituency delegates, accountable and sensitive to the views of the rank and file members. They can be quickly removed if they displease their electorate. The other two thirds represented Trade Unions and other organisations affiliated to the Labour Party, such as the Co-op Party. They are usually permanent, difficult to displace, unaccountable and remote from the influence of their members. They were the solid majority. Their ears were attuned only to Downing Street.

Frustration with the Executive among members with fully active brains had festered for decades. Virtually all decisions were made by the loyalist block without rational debate. Rarely had their decisions been of major importance, until now. The most talkative member was a retired GMB official, Terry Thomas. He was rewarded for his many services with a Blairist endorsement of his bid to become a member of the National Executive of the Party as one the Blairist 'Members First' slate.

That endorsement and the campaign that supported it marked the first stumble in Blair's total control of his flock. The Party machine backed the 'Terry Thomas' loyalist block of toadies. Over-spinning and alleged spending of £100,000 secured the election of only two of six seats for the Blairist ticket. Four of the successful candidates in the

National Executive elections were from the left-wing 'Grassroots' group. The old magic of Blair's blessing was now a liability in the eyes of many Party members. They voted for the Grassroots ticket out of pure bile against New Labour coercion. But warning impulses failed to register in New Labour's heart.

Denying their Downing Street paternity, a new group of self-appointed Welsh 'Wise Persons' emerged. Coincidentally, they were all Alun enthusiasts. A joint statement was issued in the names of: George Wright, Wales Secretary of the Transport and General Workers' Union; Don Touhig, MP for Islwyn and Spokesperson of the Taskforce assigned to choose the method to elect the leader; Wrexham Councillor Stella Matthews, Chair of Labour's North Wales Euro-constituency; and Newport Councillor Harry Jones, Chair of the Welsh Local Government Association. Their wheeze sought to anoint Alun without the bother of an election.

George Wright explained: 'The best way forward would be to have a unity ticket, involving all three people, behind which the whole of the Labour Party in Wales could unite'. The chosen trinity was to be Alun in charge, flanked by Rhodri and Wayne David as his deputies. It was compulsory unity with a threat in the tail. George said that Rhodri would 'get nothing' if he fought and lost. George's delusions of omnipotence were Promethean.

TGWU member Rhodri emoted at his leader's words. He described the ticket as a 'contemptuous' bid to make him deputy to Alun in the Labour Leadership contest. The ploy was regarded by Morgan's supporters as a crude attempt to stop Rhodri's bandwagon gaining an overwhelming momentum and to avoid a debacle for Alun. Rhodri said: 'It's entirely understandable for Alun's supporters to put out this statement because their man is so far behind me in the race that the only way he can win is if the race is called off'.

There were murmurings against the 'Wise Persons' and the might of the big Trade Union vote. Mike Smith, head of the Fire Brigades' Union in Wales, said it was 'wrong in principle that four Trade Unions should command such a large say'. George Wright, as the prime, self-appointed power-broker, made the 'Team Ticket' appeal to Rhodri to give up his leadership ambition and become Alun's deputy.

The offer to Rhodri was 'surrender now, while you're ahead'. He declined. The sensible way to avoid a major division was a deal between the two parties. Some meetings were held, but there was no meeting of minds. Downing Street had spoken. The supremacy of Alun had to be forced on a reluctant Party.

The Party was still suffering from the humiliation of the loss of its respected Leader. No-one in Wales had the appetite for another bloody feud. We ached to hear of some deal.

Other compromises were tried. The Alun camp were struck dumb when it was suggested unity could be achieved by making Alun Rhodri's deputy. Privately, and then publicly, a 'Peace Ticket' was urged. It would have put Rhodri in charge of the campaigning for the Assembly vote, with the Leadership choice left to the elected body.

The ubiquitous Peter Hain entered stage right on November 9th and called for everyone 'to take a deep breath and look at this rationally and calmly'. He said that he had suggested to Alun, on the morning of Wednesday, October 28, that he might have to run for the Welsh Labour Leadership. The next day, Ron Davies had abandoned his hopes of becoming Assembly First Secretary. Peter was unaware that he was on the brink of the most lacerating and self-destructive battle of his long campaigning life. He should have taken a deep breath.

As a counterblast to the widely believed view that Alun had sold out on devolution, Hain said his support for Alun was based on a shared conviction of the need for devolution. 'I put my authority on the line in that respect', he rashly asserted. It got worse. Peter heaped up more hostages to fortune. By mid-summer, this deft politician had drowned much of his reputation under unfulfilled predictions and an incontinence of rhetoric.

Unashamedly, he promulgated the argument that no one believed. He said:

> I would not be part of any stitch-up from London. We must consider Alun's Leadership credentials on their merits, not in the context of some hysterical and ridiculous overreaction about a stitch-up from No 10, or Alun being foisted upon the Wales Labour Party. That is simply fantasy. There will be no fixes, no attempt to deny anybody their rights.

Except the right of Rhodri to stand for the job he loved. What did Downing Street have against him to risk civil war in the Party in order to deny him a top job? That question haunted many of us who knew

Rhodri well. It still does.

The transparently dishonest excuse came up again. Rhodri does not have the Ministerial experience essential for the job. Rhodri recalled that the same argument was used by the Conservatives before the previous General Election, when no Labour politician had been a Minister for 18 years. Hardly any of the present government, including Tony Blair, had had any Ministerial experience until May 1997.

One of the few occasions when Tony Blair was left gobsmacked into silence was when Rhodri hit back at this canard and told Tony in 10 Downing Street that 'if Ministerial experience was the prime qualification, Margaret Beckett should have been sitting in that chair in 1997, not you.'

Rhodri had approached Blair and asked him if he had any problems with his bid to become Welsh Leader. Blair said he did not. The Wales on Sunday newspaper sought an explanation for the volte face a few days later. Next to a large photograph of Rhodri draped in a Welsh dragon flag they demanded a fair election and said 'all sorts of manoeuvring has clearly been going on behind the scenes and it all seems intended to stop Rhodri Morgan'. The paper asked 'Why the cold shoulder for Rhodri?' and contrasted Downing Street's original warm response to Rhodri with their subsequent portrayal of him as a dangerous maverick who must be stopped at all costs. They pointed the finger at Jack Straw, Alun's recent boss, as one of Rhodri's highly placed detractors.

A meeting of the three 'potential candidates' for the Leadership, Wayne David, Alun and Rhodri, resolved nothing, and the Taskforce that had been enlisted to select a method for choosing a Leader failed to reach any final recommendation.

Rhodri said, 'We kicked the ball around for about an hour. But if I am to stand and if Alun Michael is to stand, it is very difficult to see how you can avoid a contested election'.

In what was thought to be a pitch for popular support, Alun Michael said there was a need to take a fresh look at selections to 're-establish the partnership between the Party at the grass roots, the Party at Welsh level and the Party nationally'. That's New Labour speak for 'change the system so that I can get the job'.

Without a great deal of hope, I faxed the following to Anita Gale, the then General Secretary of the Party in Wales:

'I understand that a Taskforce will today consider the method for-electing the Leader of the Labour Group of the Welsh Assembly. As the retiring Chair of the Welsh Group of Labour MPs, I would urge the Taskforce to adopt the policy of the group to hold a one member one vote ballot. This was the strongly held opinion of our group in July.'

This is the method that has been used to elect the Leader and deputy Leader of the Party and is the most democratic and acceptable. As an election seems now inevitable, it is vital that the result should be accept-ed by the Party. The Electoral College answer is the one that lends itself to maximum influence from patronage and manipulation.

A nightmare result could be victory for one candidate in the wholly democratic constituency section but defeat by the largely undemocrat-ic Trade Union section. Personally I have always opposed an election of Leader before the Assembly itself is elected. Either the Party should postpone the election until the Assembly is elected or a one member one vote system should be adopted to ensure a result that will not lead to deepening continuing division.

Some Party members held a demonstration outside the Party's head quarters, calling for a Omov contest. Taskforce Chair Jim Hancock told the 'Omov Washes Whiter' demonstrators 'We will not be bounced into a decision'. Well, only by Downing Street.

George Wright braved the demonstration, haranguing a bearded man who appeared to be making a reasonable case. It was veteran Merthyr Party stalwart Morgan Chambers. George tartly told him he did not have to answer to non-TGWU members. The incident was shown on national television. An anti-hero was born. George was building a rep-utation for himself. Charming, gentleman George came over on televi-sion as a menacing bully. It was was not crowd pleasing. Morgan Chambers was transformed from a vaguely worried activist into an enthusiastic and energetic pro-Rhodri campaigner.

Again, George Wright argued the old theme with added hyperbole the Unions were too broke for an Omov ballot. George suggested:

We can't afford it. We have a small political fund in the Trade Union. These headstrong MPs, full of ambition, want to spend that money now. Sixty thousand letters I would have to send out and pay to get back. would break the political fund. People always want to spend the work-ers' money, including those in this contest.

George was later unavailable for comment when asked to explain th necessity for sending out 60,000 letters to Labour TGWU members in Wales when the entire Welsh Labour Party membership was, at most, 25,000. Only a small fraction of them are TGWU members.

At the time, I was not on speaking terms with the Western Mail and my name did not appear in the paper for about six months. Breaking off relations is the only protest that MPs can make when they fall out with one of the media outlets. It is no great disadvantage because there are many other sections of media in Wales in both languages for MPs to ventilate their views.

The Western Mail's importance is that it tends to set the day's agenda for broadcasters. It was oddly reassuring and comforting to know that my name would not appear in the Western Mail for six months. Nevertheless, they frequently quoted me. In this instance I was 'a Labour backbencher' who labelled Mr Wright as 'a fixer, an old-fashioned Trade Unionist' who had come up with an 'old-fashioned stitch-up which is preposterous and unacceptable'.

A realistic estimate was that sending a second class envelope to all Labour's 25,000 Welsh members would cost £5,000. The cost of a freepost return – where the Party pays only for those envelopes returned – would cost 20p per member. On a 60 per cent turnout, this would cost another £3,000. A print-run of candidates' manifestos and the ballot paper would cost another £7,000 or so, making a total of £15,000. Costs for Trade Unions would be proportional but, probably, much less because of a likely lower turnout. Small beer in Party spending. Later, Labour unearthed a war-chest of £1 million to spend on the Assembly election.

That weekend, Labour HQ staff in Cardiff were furious over a relatively minor matter. The columnist who writes under the name of 'Spin Doctor' in Wales on Sunday had called into their office and demanded a candidate's application form. It was for Alun Michael. 'Spin Doctor' thought that as a London based MP, Alun might not be able to locate the building.

It was an innocent bit of whimsy. But there were reports of spluttering rage at Transport House, proving that mild satire is more wounding than powerful polemic.

John Smith's Legacy

'One Trade Union General Secretary casting millions of votes will not happen in future'

John Smith 1993.

The Commons was buzzing with a hot bit of gossip. Alun's campaign manager, Peter Hain, had 'briefed' a journalist on the left-wing Tribune newspaper about the Taskforce's recommendation on the way the election was to be run / fixed / stitched-up. Interesting.

The Taskforce had not yet had their meeting. The Tribune journalist at first admitted he had been briefed by Peter Hain. Then he denied it.

Peter Hain vehemently rebuffed the accusation, insisting that he, possibly alone of all Welsh MPs, did not know what was planned. The next day, the Taskforce met and made the precise recommendations that appeared in Tribune that same morning and had been confidently whispered around Westminster. A breathtaking coincidence.

The favoured option was chosen in London to satisfy London's needs. It was an electoral college with the votes split three ways. One third of votes would go to the Party's 25,000 members and would be decided in a straight Omov ballot. The second third would be decided by affiliated bodies, mainly Trade Unions. Wales' four largest Unions, the GMB, TGWU, AEEU and UNISON, would have the lion's share. This section need not be conducted on the Omov basis.

This was the crucial difference from the method chosen for the Blair-Beckett Leadership contest in 1994. It eventually determined the result. For the Rhodri-Alun contest, the Taskforce and the Executive recommended only that Unions should 'consult their members as appropriate to their own rules and practices'. Oh dear.

The final third of votes went to MPs, Euro-MPs and selected Assembly candidates on the Omov basis.

It became clear that, even if Rhodri were to win majorities in two of the three sections in the college, the grassroots vote and the MPs / Assembly candidates' vote, he could still lose. The Unions were widely expected to be rigged for Alun.

Less predictable was the news that the campaign would run for three months, until February 20th. The Western Mail was assured by 'Westminster insiders' that a protracted campaign would help Alun to introduce himself to Wales outside of Cardiff, and there was a hope that Rhodri might produce a gaffe. The insiders were not named. Theories suggested that their surnames rhymed with the words twig, pain or bowels.

It brought decision day dangerously close to the May 6th Assembly vote. Would there be time to heal the wounds that were about to be deepened? Peter Hain was engineering the petard on which he was later to be sent soaring aloft.

Edith Hughes, Chair of the Party's Bridgend branch, spoke for Labour's grassroots:

This is not democracy. What's good enough for the Party Leader should be good enough for our Leader in Wales. There is something dreadfully unfair about this. The method they have chosen is heavily skewed in Alun's favour because of the block votes.

The irony was widely recognised. Old Labour Trade Union hands were firmly holding the levers of power in Wales, thanks to a New Labour fix. It was the Union vote which had made absolute Ron Davies's victory in the first ballot in September 1998, when Ron secured 92% of their votes. His victory, however, was unchallengeable because he was ahead, by smaller margins, in the other two sections with a 68% – 32% victory overall. No such emphatic victory was going to happen this time.

The Western Mail accurately observed:

The vote of each MP, Euro-MP and National Assembly candidate in the Welsh Labour Leadership election will be worth nearly 300 times an ordinary Party member's. That is one of the startling facts to emerge from the revamped electoral college. Although Labour will argue that it has introduced more democracy into this vote than first time round, a closer examination shows a less obvious shift which seems bound to help the Michael camp.

There were two subtle but crucial new fiddles. Impossible to contest was a seductive change from the Ron-Rhodri fight. Then, for speed, the General Management Committees of constituency Labour Parties made the decisions. It was not Omov by individual members. Now it was to be Omov. But this was no act of generosity, designed to be fair to Rhodri, as it was afterwards presented. It was what T S Eliot described as 'the greater treason. To do the right deed for the wrong reason'.

Those in the Alun-loop calculated that a vote by GMCs made up of Party activists would go 39 to 1 for Rhodri, the one being Alun's own constituency. An Omov ballot of all members would encompass relatively inactive New Labour leaning members who could be influenced by tabloid pressure and Blair loyalty in favour of Alun.

Secondly, in the Ron-Rhodri contest, all potential Assembly candidates had voting power equivalent to MPs. An opinion poll had found support for Rhodri among the unselected candidates running at three to one. So, a change was introduced by the Executive which disenfranchised all candidates who had not been selected for seats or for the regional lists. This was a deliberate move to reduce and distort the planned electorate in favour of Alun.

Membership of MPs / MEPs / Assembly candidates section of the electoral college had been cut from about 250 to 99. Those 99 had the voting strength of 25,000 ordinary members. Even that was not enough. There was still a real possibility of the electoral college going two to one in favour of Rhodri. Alun would be leader only by virtue of the most blatantly stitched-up Trade Union sector. So, a new fiddle was later devised to skew this section even further.

The stitchers in the Alun-loop had proved their infinite inventiveness. They were Peter Hain, Don Touhig, David Hanson and Nick Ainger. Their body language proved they were pleased with their Machiavellian handiwork. They believed they had a winning formula, but they were also to be proved to be accident prone. This was a recipe to produce an Alun victory. No one in the loop pretended that it was fair or principled.

In the summer of 1999, Tony Blair paid tribute to the memory of John Smith on the fifth anniversary of his death. Generally, the sincerity of Tony's words moved MPs in a meeting of the Parliamentary Labour Party. John was loved by the Party. The contrast between the characters of the two men was apparent when 'John's greatest legacy' was mentioned.

'We all remember John', said Tony, 'for winning for us the reform
one-member, one vote'. A sotte voce heckler was heard:

' ... and in Wales, Tony?'

'THIS NONSENSE MUST STOP!'

'Every once in a while, declare peace , it confuses the hell out of your enemies'

Ferengi Rule of Acquisition 76.

OHN PRESCOTT later apologised to me. 'I really walked straight into that one', he said. His first campaign trip to Newport is a sore memory to him.

Faithful workhorse John had been dispatched to Wales to rally the left-wing troops. His trip was into what New Labour would describe as the 'Bandit Country' of left-wing Newport. They thought the venue was in the Newport East constituency of Alan Howarth. It was woefully counter-productive and was the first of many cock-ups by the loop. Afterwards I wrote to John Prescott.

I hope you enjoyed your visit to Newport yesterday. A Party worker rang me at 5.00pm and reported that he had been contacted by Labour Party Wales and told that the meeting was for 'Party workers and not office holders'. MPs would not be welcome.

The Celtic Manor Hotel where you spoke is, and always has been, located in the ward of Caerleon. Caerleon is in Newport West. I am the MP for Newport West. With some surprise I heard at our GMC last night that the MP for Newport East had welcomed you to my constituency and that the ubiquitous Don Touhig MP was in attendance.

The arrangements for the meeting were the subject of a lively debate at Newport West GMC. As useful feedback, comments made were 'John Prescott had come along here just to give us a bollocking' and 'why was Diana Jeuda working the room so energetically to canvass support for Alun Michael?' In general the event was judged to be another sad attempt by the Party in London to ensure that their candidate avoids humiliation in the election for First Secretary of the Welsh Assembly.

Twice in the following weeks, John Prescott sought me out to expre
regret. He was not at fault. Amazingly, the MP for Newport East and th
Leader of Newport Council, Harry Jones, both thought that the Celt
Manor was in the Newport East constituency. The mistakes were ger
uine because the hotel is in the far eastern end of Newport.

I have always tried to avoid being excessively territorial about n
constituency boundaries. Generally, I invite all fellow Parliamentariar
to trample all over Newport West, if they wish. A previous MP for
Welsh seat was rumoured to mark all his borders by peeing on th
boundaries. Defending territories is a primal instinct that affects MF
Only occasionally am I miffed. Happily, I was also not invited to anotl
er escapade at the Celtic Manor.

The event amused the nation. Alun Michael and the Prince of Wal
were both caught out eating the outlawed beef on the bone. The chee
of it, coming into my constituency to consume an illegal joint. Th
definitive photograph of Alun was taken. It will pursue him for the re
of his political life. Usually it is captioned with an Alun quote that h
did not 'see any bone'. The picture showed it was a good six inche
from his nose.

Don Touhig was suddenly omnipresent. Although I was never
member of Rhodri's campaign team, the MP for Islwyn and the Labou
Party Wales Cathedral Road caucus identified me as an impediment t
the orderly progress of the stitch-up. Perhaps he had been appointed a
my personal scourge.

Don held the administrative job of Secretary of the Welsh Group c
Labour MPs. The Chair was Rhodri. Both were entitled by these office
to a place on the Welsh Executive of the Party.

Don served as bag-carrier for Gordon Brown and had an offic
strategically placed a door or two away from Tony Blair's Common
Office. His chosen role was to be seen as Tony's vicar in Wales. Withou
a nanosecond of hesitation or deviation, but with serial repetition, h
fulfilled the commands of Downing Street.

In both elections for Leader, Don was the main spokesperson for th
Taskforce and he presented himself as an objective voice of the cor
science of the Party. But he was fiercely and energetically partisan fc
Alun, in sharp contrast to his role in the Ron and Rhodri election
Ron's team released a list of supporting MPs that included Don. At th
time he was on his annual holiday in France. He issued a strong pre

release to the South Wales Argus disassociating himself from public support for Ron because, as a member of the Taskforce, he could not be seen to be taking sides. Don even took the trouble to ring Ron from the south of France to underline his objection.

There was no pretence of impartiality the second time around. Don played many roles inside and outside of the Alun-loop. The future had some unpleasant surprises for Don. His Islwyn constituency later paid the price. Months later, in answer to a question of why she and Neil were moving home from the Labour area of Islwyn to a leafy Tory village near Cardiff, Glenys asked whether Islwyn could still be called a 'Labour area'.

As keeper of the New Labour flame, Don exploded on our television screen one Saturday lunchtime to insist, with some pomposity, 'This nonsense must stop!' Quivering with anger, he announced that identical faxes had been sent to Labour Party Wales purporting to come from individual members of the Party. Shocking! Were they obscene or defamatory? No, they were pleas for a democratic electoral system or, as Don saw it, treason.

Even worse, he revealed, the faxes had been sent from the office of a Welsh MP. This was serious stuff. If an MP was using his office fax machine in this way it would be a reprehensible mis-use of Parliamentary funds.

Off camera, Don told reporters that I was the offending MP. One radio station carried the news that the source 'was an MP's office in Newport'. As the only other MP for Newport is the payroll loyal Alan Howarth, the accusation was clearly aimed at me. My crime had been reported to the Taskforce by an official of Labour Party Wales and my name was quoted.

A few days later, I confronted Don in the Members' Lobby of the Commons. He was talking to two other Welsh MPs and repeating his charge. I assured him that the log of my fax machine confirmed that no faxes had been sent on that day to Labour Party Wales. In fact, my office was not staffed. I promised Don I would get an apology out of him.

A few days later he did confess his error and so did Anita Gale. There was not an atom of truth in this manufactured story. I told them to forget about it. The matter was closed. After all, only a few hundred thousand television viewers saw the accusation. In my permanent, incurable state of optimism and benevolence, I believed that answering guilt with a kind word might encourage a little restraint from Alun's camp. Disappointment lay ahead for me.

New Labour, New Swindle

'Between the dream and the reality...Falls the shadow'
                                                    T S Eliot.

VISITORS TO STRASBOURG are regaled with a chilling tale of the power of patronage in the sixteenth century. A blasphemer was sentenced to have his tongue removed, then to be decapitated. But he shamelessly used his remaining powers of influence in high places and the sentences were reversed. He had his head cut off first.

Patronage is still widely present. There was a hope that Labour's candidates for the Assembly could be selected without the malign manipulations behind the scenes that are a cherished tradition in Wales.

One of the most able Party workers, Andrew Davies, now AM for Swansea West, devised a fresh system for selecting Assembly candidates. Several dedicated Party members laboured long and skilfully in interviewing and awarding marks to all the hopeful candidates. The objective was to produce aspirant candidates of high quality, fully representative of all the people of Wales.

But even decently laid plans can go awry. In trying to eliminate the sad, the mad and the bad, two hundred of the most loyal and able Party members were denied, probably for life, their chance of election to the Assembly. The approved list consisted of only 160 candidates.

It should have been larger because the choice of constituencies had already been restricted by the gender rules on twinning. Constituencies were sometimes voluntarily, sometimes forcibly 'twinned' with a neighbouring constituency. The joint double- constituency had to choose one male and one female candidate. The aim was to correct the ancient discrimination against women candidates in Wales. The system provoked anger and rebellion, especially from constituencies that had more favourite sons than daughters. Rhodri said 'Forced twinning of Welsh constituencies was as popular as Saddam Hussein's attempt to twin Iraq with Kuwait was - in Kuwait'

Rejected candidates were embittered. Positive discrimination had forced the choice of people who had little demonstrable loyalty or commitment to the Party. The rejection that rankled most deeply was that of Tyrone O'Sullivan, the miners' leader who led the successful campaign to save Tower Colliery and set up from scratch one of the UK's few new profitable co-operative ventures. Also out was the lifelong devolution campaigner, and potentially very able AM, Gareth Hughes. The suspicion lingers that he may have been eliminated to settle old scores.

Many rebuffed candidates hoped that they would be accepted on appeal. Poor lambs. The appeal process saw the worst practises of South Wales Labour breaking through. The omnipresent Terry Thomas was member of the three person Appeals Committee. He was the obligatory member of all committees and sub-committees of significance in Welsh Labour circles. The Appeals Committee recommended that 58 appeals be rejected and 12 allowed. Few, if any, candidates had been re interviewed. When the Appeals Committee's recommendations were presented to the group that had painstakingly interviewed and selected the original 160 candidates, they unanimously opposed the additions.

The original selection process had attempted to be a scientific, impartial one. Adding twelve 'rejects' without offering any reasons effectively destroyed the integrity of that procedure. The selection panel members were horrified that weeks of good work were to be destroyed. Finally, Terry Thomas insisted that the Appeals Committee's recommendation must be approved. They refused. He said words to the effect that, if we cannot go ahead with you, we will go ahead without you. That sounds like vintage Terry, demonstrating his version of participatory democracy.

The Appeals Committee's recommendations were later put to the Welsh Executive in Newport. I was a member at the time and raised similar objections, although I had no knowledge of the disagreement with the selection panel. I asked for the reasons why the, then, 12 candidates' appeals were to be allowed and 58 rejected. The Appeal Committee refused to give any reasons. Terry Thomas told me previously that he had been badgered by phonecalls all week.

How on earth could we, as the Welsh Executive, justify these blind recommendations? No names of new accepted candidates were ever given to the executive. 'It might be embarrassing to identify the individuals' we were told. I then asked that, even if the names were not revealed, we must be given the full reason for allowing appeals. This could be done without identifying the candidates. This was also refused.

I said that, unless some pretext was provided for these decisions, the belief would spread that those who were being added to the panel had 'friends in high places', or were the 'favourite sons or daughters' of influential people in the Party. This was denied.

It was no trivial matter. In that heap of 58 rejects, I visualised faces of women and men whom I knew well. Many of them had worked their socks off for the Party for decades during the lean, hopeless years. Of course they were worthy of being candidates. Most of them would not make it as AMs, but being denied the chance to apply was a smarting slap in the face. Some are in their late forties or fifties. There will never be another chance for them to move from full-time activism to professional politics. A rotten system had branded them as unfit to be considered as candidates.

The meeting voted to keep the details secret. Then the Executive was asked to approve the list. I voted against.

The original selection panel had given a maximum 57 marks to those candidates who had 'perfect' qualifications. They were some 'Golden Twenty' of eleven men and nine women. One member of the original election panels informs me that none of them were elected to the Assembly. Another, equally convincingly, has told me that one is now an AM and a member of the Cabinet

As part of the response to the Internet version of this book, I received this cri-de-coeur.

I feel particularly aggrieved about the result of the selection process. It was meant to be an honest and objective way of selecting candidates. But the Old Wales Labour Party 'fix-it' culture re-emerged in the appeals procedure.

The panel selection process was based on objective criteria and best practice equal opportunity principles. If it had not been done that way, Millbank would have moved in and produced something that was not as good. The outcome was good, it was certainly welcomed by the many people in the Party who believed our usual selection practices excluded them. Certainly it was flawed, but it went a long way to addressing the many concerns about the way we select candidates. The major problem was the appeals procedure, and the local constituency selection process which still favours the local Party 'barons'.

The overall result was a group of elected AMs that were similar in ability and character to those produced by the previous, discredited system. Ron had dreamed of a new democracy, with AMs drawn from outside the small, incestuous circles of Welsh Labour politics. New talents were to be attracted, from academia, business, cultural life and the media. It did not happen. At the most, one of the golden candidates got through. Others who had failed to meet the objective criteria became candidates and AMs. Reforms designed to bury nepotism had been corrupted by the endemic patronage of the Party in Wales. The Catholic Church differentiates between 'sin' and 'occasions of sin' that can lead to sin itself. The Labour Party in Wales has devised a system that create 'occasions of nepotism' that could allow malign influences to work.

I wrote to Alun saying that I had done nothing to try to reinstate the three candidates from my constituency whose appeals failed, because it would have been improper. There was evidence that others MPs and and party godfathers did intervene. Alun replied in a letter in early December 1998 that he was determined 'to correct the abuses of democracy and fair play in the Labour Party in Wales'.

That sounds a very good idea. We must try it.

ORPHAN ALUN'S ODYSSEY

'No matter how thin you slice it, it's still baloney.'
Alfred Smith

A FAVOURITE MYTH has been spun to hide the truth of the next hideous episode, Alun's Odyssey in search of an Assembly seat

In a drooling tribute to Alun Michael in July 1999, Barry Jones, Professor of Politics at Cardiff University, claims that kind-hearted Alun (which he is) refused to displace any aspirant candidate because he wanted to try a gamble on a list seat. Chapter Two of the myth is that Alun's career had peaked in the Home Office (which it had not) with the Crime and Disorder Act, so he returned to his first political love, Welsh devolution. Jones wrote that Alun decided:

> not to request a prospective Labour candidate to stand down in a safe Assembly seat but to take the more problematic route of heading a regional Party list which could have aborted his promising political career.

The magazine, The Parliamentary Monitor said in March:

> The Welsh Secretary is not assured of an Assembly seat because he was too late to be accepted for one of the 40 Welsh constituencies.

Twaddle. These articles are cogent examples of my theme that the past is always changing, even the past of less than a year ago. The truth is that those in the Alun-loop were desperately worried. It was thought that Alun's leadership bid would fail unless he persuaded a constituency to select him. The Western Mail reported an unattributable source on the mood of the hierarchy. 'The Executive is desperate to get a constituency seat for Alun and they are pushing everything through regardless of the public mood'.

The regional list seats were an arithmetical conundrum that few understood. That route was thought to be a rash gamble for a future Leader. But which constituency would have Alun? The idea that a candidate would sacrifice a seat for Alun in exchange for a peerage or a pat on the head was pure moonshine.

To get into the Welsh Assembly, Alun had to run a dangerous obstacle course. The panel of candidates, selected and augmented by patronage, had been finally closed. Without apology or explanation, the Party hierarchy decided that the firmly closed list of approved candidates should be opened to allow Alun in. Previous rejects would not be considered. Only fresh applicants were to be allowed.

In the Guardian in June 1999, Alun's camp repeated the yarn that all constituency seats had been selected when Ron Davies resigned. So Alun had no choice but the dangerous lottery of a list seat. The proof of that untruth is Jane Davidson. An ex-researcher of Rhodri's, Jane was not on the panel in October. She was one of the successful new applicants. She secured the Pontypridd nomination and is now an AM and Deputy Presiding Officer of the Assembly.

Jane was interviewed for the panel on the same day that I was. That was when I played my tiny role in this drama. Originally, deciding not to stand for the Assembly was a difficult decision, one which I may regret. As the panel was re-opened and I was not previously a candidate, I could now apply. I put my name in, partly to give me more time to reconsider the joys of life in Cardiff Bay, but mainly to stop Alun.

I shared the anger of many Party members when stalwart MP Dennis Canavan was rejected from the panel in Scotland because of his left-wing record. That decision boomeranged back on Scottish Labour when Dennis won the biggest majority of any candidate in Scotland as an Independent Labour MSP. I half expected to be rejected in the same way that Dennis Canavan had been because my Blairist deference was not always whole hearted. Not so. The panel oozed charm and put me on the list.

Westminster or the Assembly was always a knife-edge decision for me. Having marched through Cardiff in 1953 from Cardiff Castle to today's Welsh Office carrying a Labour Party sign reading 'A Parliament for Wales', I longed to be a part of the Welsh Assembly. But devolution had come later in my life than I expected. With my family, I decided that the most sensible plan was to try for another term in Westminster where I had found a niche. Offering myself at retirement age to a brand new Assembly was an option that may well have been judged unacceptable to the Party and voters.

But I was incensed that the tentacles of Blairist control-freakery were out to impose a compliant, unimaginative leader on our fledging democracy. My main purpose was to prevent a constituency nomination for Alun. I announced that I would stand in any constituency where Alun offered himself as a candidate. An unnamed spokesperson from Alun's camp snarled back at me in the South Wales Echo.

My hope was to expose the woeful level of support among grassroots members for Alun. Personal preferences aside, I was confident that if the choice was between me as True Labour and Alun as New Labour, True Labour would win. Loyalty to Alun or Rhodri was becoming a key factor in selections all over Wales.

It was a worrying period. My comfortable existence might have been disrupted if I became the candidate and later AM for a part of Wales beyond my beloved Newport. My campaigning from Westminster on a host of issues would be prematurely ended. Happily, my family went along with it and prayed that Alun would not try for a constituency.

Fighting my own seat was not an option and I had told my constituency. Rosemary Butler and John Griffiths had been adopted to fight Newport West and East respectively, bringing up to 8 the total of 40 seats that had selected candidates by early December 1998.

Informed gossip and news reports agreed that Alun's best chance of a constituency seat was Blaenau Gwent. Local MP and arch anti-devolutionist Llew Smith appeared to be beckoning him. Llew had enthusiastically backed Rhodri in his contest with Ron. He at first said he was undecided on his choice between Rhodri and Alun. As with many political decisions, this was a choice of which candidate Llew disliked the least.

He was not a natural ally of either. Rhodri was too Welsh for him: Alun too right-wing. Significantly, Llew's support for Alun was announced on the same day as that of Neil Kinnock and Alan Williams, MP for Swansea West. The most irksome opponents of devolution in 1979, 1997 and in Parliament were united in backing the candidate they thought was weaker on devolution. Their backing mangled Alun's claim to be an earnest disciple of devolution.

The young Neil Kinnock was famously remembered for allegedly telling Leo Abse on Callaghan's devolution for Wales Bill in 1979 that 'With your money Leo, and my brains, we can beat this thing'. They did.

Alan Williams is a London based MP who eccentrically argued that MPs with homes outside Wales should have no vote in the Ron-Rhodri contest because they personally would not be affected by the outcome. Alan had a unique phobia at the prospect of local Councillors taking decisions on a Wales level that he judged to be the province of MPs.

A beguiling footnote that confirms the quixotic nature of political loyalty is the fact that Llew Smith and Alan Williams (Swansea West) were two of only six MPs to declare themselves as Rhodri's supporters in his battle with Ron. Now, a few months later, they were among his most ardent foes.

A dazzling new truth was emerging. Previously, the principled decision was to vote for Omov. Now, the principled choice was to vote against Omov. This was the birth of a new left-wing political nostrum. Was this the Third Way ? No, it is the tenth precept of Pompomism: 'Select the desired outcome and adjust your principles to achieve it'.

But it was not just Llew's legendary lobbying of his own Party that made Alun optimistic. How Llew canvassed for Alun remains a tormenting mystery of Welsh politics. Did he say, 'back Alun because he is a right-wing, Welsh-speaking Cardiffian, a devolutionist who planned to deny North Gwent its own Health Trust'? Or, was it 'Alun is less enthusiastic about devolution than Rhodri. What's more, he's big in the Co-op Movement'. The latter is more likely.

Blaenau Gwent is one of the few places in Wales that could be described as a hotbed of Co-operative Party activity. Alun was an adopted Co-op MP, the Co-op Party's favourite Welsh son. Could they now find a home for Orphan Alun? The two other male candidates tipped in the seat, Peter Law and Ian Janes, were also members of the Co-operative Party. Its rules state that they would both have to stand down if another Co-op choice was nominated by the constituency.

It is ironic that the man who had achieved more in practically implementing the 'Co-operative Ideal' than all Co-op Party members combined was Tyrone O'Sullivan. He had already been deemed unworthy to be considered as a candidate.

There was a third factor. Blaenau Gwent was also seething with resentment at the twinning process that Rhodri backed. They were one of four constituencies which had refused to take part in the process of ensuring equal numbers of male and female candidates. The Wales Labour Party had taken the organisation of the selection process out of the hands of the local Party. Could the Party apparatchiks stitch up the selection for Alun?

Blaenau Gwent had other ideas. The constituency Party Secretary, Liz Pleece, announced that Alun, Rhodri and the third potential candidate, Roger Warren Evans, would be setting out their wares at a full Party meeting in Ebbw Vale. It was a hustings meeting in which all members could hear and question the candidates.

Roger Warren Evans was a worthy but unexpected contender. He had been a Party member for 35 years. He said he was standing to open up the contest. 'I believe the leadership should be open to all Party members. This must be a real election', he said. His candidature was a bit a mystery. A moderate on all issues, he presented himself as a Swansea nationalist in that he was neither a Cardiff nor a Westminster man. Not that that did him much good. He was a predictable poor third in Blaenau Gwent.

Roger overflows with praise for the original list selection process and he told me that 'the three hustings I attended in Barry, Pontypool and Ebbw Vale were a credit to the Party, well-attended, well-managed and courteous'. But Roger failed to gain the essential two nominations from Unions, partly because his own GMB Union did not nominate and only the MSF invited him to set out his stall for them.

Although the result in Ebbw Vale was wounding to Roger, it was a knock-out blow for Alun. He was beaten three to one by Rhodri. The standing of Llew Smith and the Co-op Party also took a hammering. The vote was by the same electorate that would choose the Assembly candidate for Blaenau Gwent.

At the same time, there was another battering. Peter Hain's constituency nominated Rhodri Morgan. This was in spite of Peter's operatic entreaties that this move would be embarrassing to him. He was to Alun what Waylon Smithers is to Monty Burns. The constituency had robustly taken a line that was independent of Peter. The honeymoon was over. There were stories of unprecedented, angry scenes in the Neath constituency between MP and activists.

Alun was in trouble. If he could not swing a decent vote in a seat where he had the MP and the Co-op Party sewn up, he had no chance anywhere. He knew that if there were no other opponents, I had publicly vowed to stand against him in any seat he chose. There was no constituency left which would not have selected True Labour instead of Alun's tarnished New Labour. It was the end of his hopes of representing a constituency. Only the undemocratic list seats were left. They were almost entirely in the gift of the Party machine. The only list seat where Labour had a good chance of winning was that of Mid and West Wales, corresponding to the Euro-constituency boundaries of Eluned Morgan's seat.

It was Hobson's choice. The ever faithful Nick Ainger set the stage in Carmarthen to announce that Alun was to be a list candidate in Mid and West Wales. On December 20th, the day before the announcement, the Wales on Sunday newspaper upstaged Alun's news management strategy. They described the planned move as an act of desperation forced on Alun because of his inability to secure a constituency seat.

The Welsh Office based Alun-loop agonised. How could they make this panic driven last gasp choice sound like a decision of calculated policy?

A brainstorming session accepted the suggestion from, it is rumoured, Jon Owen Jones, to spin the story with the help of the ancient Welsh tales of the Mabinogion. Bendigeidfran was king of Britain and led his army to Ireland to avenge a slight to his sister Branwen. He spanned the sea between Wales and Ireland using his own body as a bridge across which his soldiers marched. Alun announced his decision, describing Mid and West Wales as the bridge between the other parts of the nation. 'There is a Welsh saying: a leader should be a bridge. Bid pen, bid pont,' he bilingualised. 'Born in North Wales and serving a constituency in Cardiff, I am conscious that Labour's leader in the Assembly needs to unite the sometimes disparate needs of our country'.

He said he had been asked to apply for half a dozen constituency seats but 'did not want to push aside strong local candidates whose talents we need in the Assembly'. Undiluted, 100%, copper-bottomed baloney. For one thing, Bendigeidfran was a giant.

Even his supporters, gathered in Carmarthen for the event, could not avoid being visibly embarrassed. Labour's opponents took advantage. Future AM Helen Mary Jones, who topped Plaid Cymru's Mid and

West list, said 'It's not an area he's got any obvious links with. I can only guess that it smacks of desperation and he is having even more difficulty finding a first-past-the-post seat than we thought.'

Chris Lines of the Lib-Dems said, 'The Labour Party has got itself into an almighty mess. He (Alun) would be representing one part of Wales in one Parliament, another part in another Parliament. Labour is devaluing the basis of the Assembly'.

No-one believed the spin. This was an obvious, transparent admission that Alun had failed to win over the grassroots of the Labour Party. He mystified an audience of hacks by announcing another compelling justification for morphing into a bridge: 'My Grandmother was a Seamstress in Llanrhaedr-ym-Mochnant'.

Another irony not observed at the time is that Alun has been a life-long opponent of Proportional Representation. His experience of Germany's political system, gleaned as a result of the Cardiff-Stuttgart twinning link, had convinced him that PR had caused the unequal and malign influence of the Free Democrats in Germany. PR had won them a permanent place in governments for decades. He had long defended first past the post and denounced PR. Astonishingly, he returned to this theme after the election. He again attacked the ladder which allowed him to reach a place in the Welsh Assembly.

The list strategy was a gamble that could have proved ruinous. Alun was up-beat because Party number-crunchers had convinced him that Labour was a shoe-in for at least one list seat in the Mid and West Wales region. The mechanism for calculating winners under the list system is fiendishly complex. Even Alun appeared to be in the dark and repeatedly said his team of advisers had done their arithmetic.

A leviathan of a shock lay in wait.

'CRACHACH-RACY'

'We are not interested in the possibilities of defeat, they do not exist'
Queen Victoria 1899

RHODRI had a substantial lead in two key battlefields when nominations closed. Among constituency Labour parties, Rhodri had 20 nominations against Alun's eight. Of the Assembly candidates, Rhodri had 57 nominations to Alun's 32.

Optimism was compulsory from both camps. Rhodri said he was the people's choice. Alun's camp said the momentum was with their man. Of course.

Rhodri had further good news. Surveys showed him well ahead. A telephone poll gave him 84 per cent to the Welsh Secretary's 16 per cent. A poll in the South Wales Echo recorded 1,754 votes for Rhodri, and 334 for Alun.

Rhodri told a press Conference:

> *I give you my personal guarantee that under my leadership the Assembly will be free of sleaze, free of patronage, and free of machine politics. I promise 'Cynulliad y werin, nid Cynulliad y crachach' - an Assembly of the people, not of the establishment.*

'Crachach' literally means a scab that forms on a wound. It's pronounced like the sound of a bronchitic spitting into a fire. It's a term of mild abuse used to described the elite, the posh, the upper class.

There were four unexpected Christmas crackers waiting for Alun.

The first was close to home. Rachel Lomax, Permanent Secretary at the Welsh Office, announced that she was jumping ship. It was completely unexpected. She was an enthusiast for devolution and had recently bought a house in the Cowbridge area.

Previously, she had spurned a tempting job offer from the pounding heart of Blairism, the Downing Street Policy Unit. It was not plausible that she now found the charms of the Department of Social Security irresistible.

She wanted to oversee the takeover of power, from Welsh Office to Assembly. Her relationship with Ron Davies had been good. He affectionately called her Mrs Merton. She had described the effect of his departure on the Welsh Office as like 'falling off a cliff'.

In a profile in the magazine Planet in October 98, Stephen Evans says that Rachel had no plans to move. 'I may be here for ever and a day', she told him. Evans wrote, 'That assertion ought to please us'. Indeed it did. Evans was only one amongst a harmonious Hallelujah Chorus of praise from Wales for the talents of Rachel. Ron and Rachel were the dream godparents to attend the birth of the Assembly.

The official Welsh Office line was that there was absolutely no conflict with Alun. Others claimed that Alun had problems in relating to Welsh Office staff. In his election campaign in 1987, a perceptive reporter said that his campaign was a winning one, but there was an impediment. Alun thought he was the agent: the agent, Jack Brooks thought he was the candidate.

Civil servants at the Home Office shuddered at the sight of Alun with his clipboard extended, bearing down on them in corridors. He was obsessed with details that they thought were their business. Could it be that the Minister thought he was a civil servant and Rachel Lomax thought she was a Minister?

Rhodri echoed the general suspicion.

The timing is extremely inconvenient for the devolution process, not to say a little odd. From my contacts with Rachel Lomax, she has up until now expressed a view strongly that Wales is where the action is and she wanted to stay here to supervise the transition to the Assembly and then for a year or so afterwards.

The second embarrassment was self-inflicted from Alun's accident prone campaign manager. The uncomfortable bit of news was Peter Hain's admission that his staff broke Parliamentary rules by using House of Commons post to send letters to Party members, begging them to back Alun for the Welsh Labour Leadership.

Hain's curious excuse was that the letters were in the same envelopes as Christmas cards posted by Mr Hain's office to leading members of his local Party. The press did not latch on to the double error. Christmas cards should not be sent in Commons envelopes. It's the only mail for which MPs must provide their own stamps. Overdosing on puns, Kevin Brennan said 'if Alun's team want to come to us for frank advice on how to lick this problem we'll be pleased to help them stamp it out'.

The third blow robbed the Assembly and Alun of a a valuable future AM. Alun's supporters were losing badly at grassroots and proof came with the rejection of sitting North Wales MP Gareth Thomas in his own seat in Clwyd. He applied to be the Assembly candidate as an Alun backer. He was defeated by the little known Alan Pugh who supported Rhodri. This was very worrying news for Alun. Gareth is a first class MP and the Clwyd West constituency Labour Party is typical of most in Wales.

While Alan Pugh is an able AM, but the loss of someone who is an enthusiast for devolution and a speaker of the Welsh Language from the cradle has left a glaring gap in the ranks of AMs. It was a further price that the party was paying for the imposed will of Downing Street. Candidates were being select less on their merits and more one whether there were in Alun's or Rhodri's camp.

At the same moment, one of the minor early stitch-ups was being un-picked. Parachuted in Euro candidate Lyndon Harrison stood down from the North Wales seat for 'health reasons.' It was consoling in June to hear that Lyndon's health was robust enough for him to take on the tiring job of a working peer. Cynics smiled knowingly. Future events proved that Lyndon had taken the best course. The electorate were to give their judgment on whether a third Labour MEP should represent Wales. Not all elections can be stitched-up.

The fourth blow was caused by Alun stepping outside of his usual character. Alun, the circumspect did something rash. He was accused of being grossly premature in making what appeared to be an offer of a Cabinet job in the National Assembly to Ron Davies.

Alun had said in a statement that he thought Ron's talents would be needed and would be used in the Assembly. Later, he back-tracked, say-ing 'I'm not offering people jobs. This could only happen once the Assembly elections were over'. But Tories denounced him for 'cashing political blank cheques on his self-important belief that he is the only choice for Wales '.

Rhodri commented that 'This is the type of old-fashioned machine politics that we are trying to get away from. It's grossly premature'. The Western Mail speculated that there was a plot for Alun to serve as Welsh Secretary for a year or two then return to his natural habitat in the Home Office, handing the leadership over to Ron Davies, who by then might have been fully rehabilitated.

That idea, too, collapsed in bitterness, humiliation and tears. As someone cruelly said, 'rehabilitation is a process, not an event'.

On the 27th December, Wales on Sunday published what looked like an insignificant story unconnected with the leadership race. Davie Lewis, the top official in Wales of GPMU, the print Union, was suspended without pay for two months following alleged irregularities in a Union election that saw him confirmed in his job. The paper's 'Spin Doctor' said that during his suspension he had been invited to Downing Street to the reception for Welsh Party members and commented 'Purdah, as Peter Mandelson has discovered, is not a word in the Blair Lexicon.'

Peter had his own troubles at that time. Proving that one side still had a sense of humour was a letter on official notepaper to Peter Hain allegedly written by Peter Mandelson who now had time on his hands. Inter alia it said:

> 'Tony is worried that Alun is stuck up sludge creek in a leaky coracle. Perhaps you should pass him the bargepole that you wouldn't touch this job with?
>
> Get rid of the suntan, Pete. Standing next to you, Alun looks even more like corpse. Rhodri has not only swallowed all this bollocks about democracy, he has persuaded some of the Taffies to do the same. Do your best Peter, otherwise you will make us a laughing stock. As you know, that is my job.
>
> Regards, Peter M

There's Tidy

'I am a brother to dragons and a companion to owls'

Proverbs 30:29

THE FIXERS fixed, the writers scribbled, the Welsh Labour Party declared war on itself.

Writing in the Guardian, Roy Hattersley said:

> *Two of Labour's deepest instincts are at war. One is the commitment to spread power around, the other the urge to keep every last shred of it to itself. The good angel knows it should devolve power, the bad, control-freak angel can't let go.*

The logic of devolution is that power should no longer be concentrated in Whitehall ... now that it comes to picking the people to implement that principle, the principle itself is trampled on. Stitching up Rhodri will anger the already restless loyalists of Welsh Labour. devolution was never a done deal in Wales, and motivation levels will sink low next May if activists are forced to knock on doors for a leader they did not choose.

Many others were haunted by the doleful prospects of the nemesis to come. In my weekly column in the South Wales Echo, I made a final plea in an open letter:

> *Dear Alun,*
> *Please do some hard thinking. Only you can stop the election campaign that nobody wants. There are two possible results - both bad for you, Wales and the Labour Party.*
>
> *You could win a Pyrrhic victory with the votes of the undemocratic Union and pay-roll MPs' votes, while Rhodri wins the democratic votes*

of members. You would be leader without honour.

The alternative is even worse. Yet, you may still lose. That would be humiliation. Rhodri' s huge lead in the poll in this paper confirms all other evidence that he is the the runaway favourite. If you are not convinced, take a stroll down Queen Street tomorrow morning.

You will be greeted with some friendly nods, smiles and the occasional handshake. Then follow Rhodri on the same route. He will be mobbed by happy cheering Cardiffians of all parties. Rhodri is the choice of the people of Wales .

Your friends, that still includes me, have applauded your deserved charmed life in politics. You have been fairly promoted because of your fine work. Recent events have in your words 'bruised' you. If the scrap between you and Rhodri goes ahead, it can only get bitter.

There is a third alternative which I have been urging on you for weeks now. There is still time for you to pull out of this election. Accept Rhodri as the Leader of the campaign. The choice of Leader of the Labour Group in the Assembly can then be made by the elected Assembly members. Then we can get on with the task of creating our new Welsh Democracy.

That drew some vitriolic abuse from a reader who picturesquely described me as a person who 'vomited a column every week'. The letter had literary merit absent from the Echo's usual one from 'Disgusted of Splott.' Was this a production from Alun's professional team of New Labour acolytes? From a previous experience in 1995, I know, that is the way they operate.

My column is invisible to the majority of my constituents who are devoted to the South Wales Argus. But the Echo provides a wonderful platform for me to address the influential capital city of Cardiff readership. It gave me a chance to contribute my inside knowledge on one of the oddest suggestions for Blair's rejection of Rhodri. Roy Hattersley wrote,

Nothing now surprises me about New Labour. So when I read that Tony Blair had been offended by the sight of Rhodri's untidy living room, I was perfectly prepared to believe that Alun is the Prime Minister's choice to lead the Welsh Assembly because he regularly plumps up the cushions on his sofa.

Many others were baffled. Rhodri certainly has a personality that can make the insecure and orthodox feel uncomfortable. He had difficulty fitting into the expected persona of an MP. He was interviewed on television the day after his victory wearing jeans and a lumberjack shirt. At Cardiff station, on our first visit to London after our election in 1987, he was puzzled. I had moved out of the sight of the Echo photographer the Tesco plastic bags in which he was carrying his smalls. 'What did you do that for?', he asked. Not for years did he acknowledge the expectation of many voters that their MPs should look like toffs.

There was an unexpected sequel when I recently posted that story on my website. An e-mail winged its way to me through cyberspace from a long-standing member of Rhodri's staff:

You've solved the great unanswered question. How the hell did Rhodri lose his new shirts and Tesco bags on Cardiff station? I know he had them when I left him at the station. It was because you moved them so that the Echo Photographer could not see them. The upshot of all this was that Rhodri phoned me at home at 11.30pm and I had to go to the station to find his 'luggage'. I found them in lost property labelled 'I think these belong to an MP'.

Still, I got my own back when I phoned him at his flat at 1.00 am and told him that they would be on the first train from Cardiff in the morning. 5.30am.

It's bad news for Tesco, but, since being elevated to the Welsh Assembly, Rhodri has invested in a couple of suitcases, I am reliably informed.

Untidiness was almost obligatory in the 30 feet by 12 feet room into which Rhodri, Alun, Paul Murphy, Elliott Morley, John MacFall, Eric Illsley and I were crammed in our first term in Parliament.

The space in the office shrank quickly. Researchers were expected to share a corner of the single desks we each had. Alun was an inveterate territory-expander. He assembled his work in piles on the floor. They rapidly spread, filling all the empty spaces between the desks. Rhodri's 'guilt' heaps of un-read reports grew in pillars on his desk until he disappeared behind them.

Three years after we first arrived, Rhodri's new researcher, the now AM Jane Davidson, dismantled the columns. By then, they were four foot high. They marked the passage of time in a similar way to the rings of a tree. Three inches down was 'December 89', another foot lower, 'September 88'.

If tidiness was the main qualification for First Secretary of the Welsh Assembly, Paul Murphy would be Blair's choice. Paul's desk incited feelings of homicide. He is pathologically tidy. Not only was there never a piece of paper on his desk, but he regularly polished it. It mockingly gleamed at our shared chaos.

Signs of the antagonism to come cast their shadows. Differences between Rhodri and Alun over the Cardiff Bay Barrage Bill introduced tension into an already claustrophobic habitat. Rhodri, Alun and I had previously combined to buy equipment. Neither Rhodri nor Alun had experience of divorce. When they fell out there were serious difficulties. How do you cut a fax machine in half? Who would have custody of the Young Socialists?

Rhodri believes that Blair was greatly influenced by the night that he spent in his Michaelston-le-Pit home. Tony rose early in the morning to write a speech for the Vale of Glamorgan by-election. Unexpectedly, an elderly relative of Rhodri's wife Julie, who had been sleeping in an out-building, wandered in and said 'I know who you are … You're that Lionel Blair'.

Strangely, the only office and house in Wales that are reputed to be even more untidy than Rhodri's are Alun's. When we all acquired our own offices, Alun's won a legendary reputation as the Commons' tip. I believe it was Alun who finally could take no more of Paul Murphy provocative neatness and decorated his desk with the sign 'A tidy desk is proof of a diseased mind'.

If only Blair had recognised that truth.

MISSING THE PEOPLE

'Treat people in your debt like family. Exploit them'
Ferengi Rule of Acquisition No.111.

ALUN embarked on a trek across Wales.

He had three months to introduce himself to the Labour Party beyond Cardiff. Optimistically named the 'Meet the People' tour, it was derided as the 'Miss the People' tour.

Turnout varied from 5 in Barry, to 120 in Cwmbran, when Alun was demoted to the 'B feature' because the much loved Mo Mowlam starred.

Civil servants were present at his first meeting at Newport Civic Centre and Alun was chauffeured there in full Secretary of State mode. Could this be judged to be a legitimate use of public money? I wrote to Rachel Lomax and enclosed a copy of a South Wales Argus report. The pre-publicity clearly said that this was part of Alun's effort to secure his Leadership victory. Lomax defended her position. She had no choice. She wrote that the tour was 'not a party event. The support provided by the Department has been part of its normal duties and has been met from existing resources.' It is unlikely that tour did Alun much good but an examination of the whether the line between use of public money and civil service staff throughout the campaign would produce some alarming evidence.

The audiences were embarrassingly tiny except when a star from the Cabinet was present. The effect was not helpful to the eclipsed Alun. He often looked outclassed by fellow Cabinet members with giant person-alities. Alongside Gordon Brown he looked like a teenaged son asking Dad for a loan of the car keys. One revealing incident occurred in Cwmbran.

The Observer's Demon Ears heard all:

The oldest of Old Labour fixes is on in Wales to stop the off-message (aka human) Rhodri Morgan leading the Labour group in the Welsh Assembly. But even the all-powerful Taffia cannot turn Alun Michael, Millbank's anointed candidate, into a charismatic politician. It's the Welsh Secretary's temper, you see, boys, however hard you try you can't get him to find it, let alone direct it at deserving targets.

The other day the magnificent Mo Mowlam went to Wales and Colette Hume, a local hackette, was assigned to interview her. She had heard that busy Mo allowed female journalists to grab a few minutes with her in the ladies, but when she mentioned the idea to Michael he went into ballistic orbit and told her not to approach Mowlam.

Hume ignored Michael, as so many do, and nipped into the lavs after Mo, but failed to pluck up the courage for an interview. She emerged to face a furious reception. Alan Cummins, Michael's press officer, said the Minister had hit the roof. 'I've never seen him so angry before. You've done your career and reputation a great deal of harm. Christ almighty, it was disgraceful behaviour'. An understandably nervous Hume approached Mowlam, who didn't seem in the least upset.

Hume: 'Can you please get me out of the dog-house, it was me who followed you into the loo?'

Mowlam: 'Don' t worry about it, people get officious.'

Hume: 'The problem is that they' re going a bit barmy, so if I get shouted at . The Welsh Office lot were going mad.

Mowlam: Tell the Welsh Office to piss off.'

At this point Mo in a voice which has made some of Europe's worst terrorists tremble booms: 'ALUN.' Alun Michael stomps over:

'Colette came into the loo because I often talk to women in the loo.'

Michael (turning puce): 'She asked if it was all right and was told no. It's appalling.'

Mowlam: 'Hmmm. Well, it's unfair for her to be in trouble over that.'

Now (to Michael who is now beet root) Would you pass me a glass of water and (to Hume, who is now smug) we'll get talking. Go on, Colette...'

Knowing well all four people involved in this anecdote, and after some careful checks, I can vouch for the absolute accuracy of that story. Colette Hume had arranged to interview Mo long before the meeting. Further to the Observer, it was heartwarming to hear that Colette did ask her questions in the loo and wrote a splendid piece about it.

Once more, Alun's short fuse of petulance had blown. Although Rhodri was being maligned as an unsafe pair of hands, it's Alun who has the explosive temper. Unfortunately, he sometimes loses some of his dignity with his temper.

The most cringing public display of this came in a Newsnight interview with Jeremy Paxman. All politicians are rightly wary of being barbecued by the Master Inquisitor. Ministers now routinely dodge interviews for fear of suffering the humiliation of Michael Howard who was asked the same question a dozen times, which he memorably answered with a dozen evasions.

Alun is a thoroughly experienced television performer. As a Minister, he had lived in the relatively sheltered waters of the Home Office. There were few real taxing press challenges. It was an easy ride, standing in the shadow of Jack Straw, promoting the government's view that crime is a bad thing and stopping crime is a good thing.

But Paxman, rampant and audacious, floored him. The questions were hostile but reasonable. Alun was tense, argumentative, repetitive and woefully unconvincing.

The final image that lodged in the viewers' minds was of Alun answering Jeremy's 'thank you, Mr Michael' with a snarling, sarcastic AND THANK YOU, too'. He tore off his lapel microphone, flung it away and flounced out of the picture.

Sensitive supporters of Alun probably wept. They recalled Rhodri's relaxed performance and his startling waterfowl imagery on the same programme. There was no way to spin Alun's calamity.

Democracy Comrades, But Not as we Know it

'One of the great achievements of New Labour, is the almost total destruction of dissent'

Roy Hattersley

Not so in Wales. The stitch-ups had provoked dissent to raise its lovely, familiar Welsh head. In early January 1999, the Party's war with itself looked towards a possible split after May 7th.

The Western Mail reported that 'a senior Labour Party figure, a former member of the Welsh Executive, believes there is a growing groundswell of discontent of over London-centred policies being foisted upon Wales'. There was even talk of a possible new 'Radical Labour Party'. The 'senior Labour Party figure' went on to say 'London is dictating our agenda and we would have to look again at how to take control of Welsh politics. That would mean a new Party'.

The identity of the un-named senior figure was immediately identifiable to all the cognoscenti of Welsh Labour. He was thought to be a justifiably embittered lone voice, with little influence and no following. There was understanding because he was a lifelong worker for devolution who had been unfairly blackballed for his views and excluded from the Assembly selection process.

Scenting a weakness, Peter Hain went nuclear. He hit back at what he called the 'splitters'. There was only one. Undeterred, he went on, 'they should join Plaid Cymru if they have such contempt for Labour's democratic processes'.

Democratic? Many of the Labour Party faithful were aghast. Is this the best shot at democracy we are going to get? They did not join Plaid Cymru, but later they abstained or voted Plaid in huge numbers. Peter's comments deepened the disillusionment.

There was worse to come. Peter extended the argument to Rhod
and his supporters, saying,

I have been very alarmed about what Rhodri Morgan said abou
wanting an autonomous Wales Labour Party and his most active sup
porters pursuing a crypto-nationalist agenda.

If there are those among his supporters, as there now appear to b
who won't accept a democratic outcome and split off and form a ne
Party that betrays a massive fault line running through the middle of h
campaign. It's not a left or right issue; it's an issue about separatism.

Alun had previously seized on Rhodri's call for Welsh Labour Part
autonomy. Although it was a repeat of a very similar call by Alun, Pete
distorted Rhodri's idea as blood curdling nationalist threat. He the
attacked the distortion that he had created. The argument was insultir
to the mass of Rhodri's supporters and deeply divisive.

In an article months later, the Western Mail's Mike Settle revealed th
he had been told before the campaign had started that Alun's tea
intended to paint Rhodri as a crypto-nationalist. The unequal spread
malice on Rhodri's side was proved by his failure to ever denounc
Alun and Peter as former Liberals.

The wide gulf in the Party was on visible display at a soiree in 1
Downing Street. It was an unprecedented bash thrown by Tony Blai
presumably to promote Alun. Both factions were invited.

It was as comradely as a joint meeting of Celtic and Rangers sup
porters. Rhodri's chums flocked to one end of the room, Alun's clu
tered at the other. Tony and Cherie occupied the no-man's-land in th
middle, vainly trying to broker a truce. A minor accident with a tra
door later that evening left Rhodri with a black eye. With difficulty, I
convinced the hacks it was not the result of a punch-up between th
two camps.

Union chiefs were also getting stuck into the wine and cheese
Downing Street that night. The AEEU vote was due in Swansea th
next day. By an extraordinary coincidence, Deputy Prime Minister Joh
Prescott, Foreign Secretary Robin Cook and Northern Irelar
Secretary Mo Mowlam were also all in Swansea on the same day f
Labour's National Policy Forum. Not to be left out, Tony Blair was vi
iting North Wales, his second Alun-boosting trip.

In the early part of the day, Rhodri visited some of his groupies
Tower Colliery. He rejected the invitation to condemn Blair's trip. 'A

is fair in love, in war and in politics' he said. This absolution was extended to a tactic Rhodri described as 'trying to nobble' the AEEU vote by a 'desperate mis-use of a list of delegates that Peter Hain was phoning'. Rhodri had not been allowed to use the list. He said he was a winner, not a whinger, but demanded equal treatment from the Unions.

Hain knee-jerked back and described Rhodri's accusations as 'smears and ridiculous allegations which are groundless'. But he did not deny having the list and making the calls.

Wales on Sunday reported the indignation of one AEEU member.

I am a member of the Swansea Branch. We have 4,000 members yet we do not have a delegate to this committee and the leadership issue has never been discussed at a branch meeting.

Both sides were making round the clock use of telephone canvassing. Peter Hain and Don Touhig were hyperactive. Their patter was tentative. They suggested to the doubtful that Rhodri was an 'unsafe pair of hands', 'lovely chap to have a drink with, but no judgment, y'know'. He was variously portrayed as a 'loose cannon', a 'crypto-nationalist' and 'anti-Westminster'. As Kevin Morgan wrote, 'if he were a loose cannon it is a mystery how Neil Kinnock, John Smith and Tony Blair appointed him to the shadow Front Bench'.

Rhodri's line was more straightforward. 'We are being shafted by New Labour from London'. Rhodri's team suffered from a lack of guile. They were genuinely shocked by the fusillade of dirty tricks hurled at their candidate. They came from all directions. Rhodri rarely shows anger, but one day he stormed into my office at 1 Parliament Street. He had just had faxed to his office, on the same floor as mine, a letter sent by Councillor Harry Jones, the Leader of Newport County Borough Council. Dated January 12 and on Council notepaper was a plea for help from Alun's camp from former Welsh Party Chair Terry Thomas. Who else?

The letter read:

Basically, Terry is asking group leaders to identify Councillors within each group they represent, who would be prepared to draw up a list of people who are uncommitted to either of the leadership candidates or others who could be persuaded to 'cross over'.

Mr Thomas will arrange for someone to contact the various parties in an attempt to influence them to a favourable stance in support of Alun.

Rhodri fairly described this as a blow below the belt. Ineptly, the letter was to a former Council leader, David Edwards, who had already nominated Rhodri in the leadership race. The official Labour Party line was supposed to be neutral. He was incensed by the letter and the alleged stance of Newport County Council. Did they know their notepaper was being used?

Harry Jones, leader of Newport Council and chair of the Welsh Local government Association, said:

I understand the vast majority of Labour leaders in Wales have, as individuals, declared for Alun Michael. On that basis, I am contacting them to set up a network and send out leaflets.

He had a prior arrangement to pay the postage, etc, to Newport County Borough Council, in the same way that Peter Hain had made prior arrangements to pay the Serjeant at Arms for postage of his Christmas cards.

The vast majority of Newport Labour members backed Rhodri. The Councillors had never discussed it. On whose behalf was Harry appealing?

Rhodri's anger was expressed in a complaint about the abuse of the elections procedures. Only simple 500 word statements were allowed for each candidate. Now, according to an article in the Daily Post Alun's camp had sent out thousands of leaflets with accompanying letters from MPs to Party members in 20 constituencies. There were several other allegations that Alun's team were breaking the rules.

It was Democracy comrades, but not as we know it.

Out of the Bowels

'The Labour Party emerged out the bowels of the Trade Union movement'

Ernest Bevin.

EVIN'S scatological image is, perhaps, the one most Welsh Trade Union Godfathers have of the Welsh Labour Party.

A titanic struggle was going on behind the scenes. Trade Unions were training their muscles to push their favourite candidates. Both sides said they had spies working in their opponent's camp. There were far more men and women press-ganged into serving Alun by their Trade Unions than Rhodri because of Rhodri's majority grassroots support.

Certainly, Rhodri anticipated many moves by Alun's faction. The conspiracies rolled on. It is a mistake to believe this was one giant stitch-up. It was a vast blanket woven from thousands of minor stitch-ups, weaved together in every corner of Wales. A large proportion of Union staff, computers and fax machines were beavering away to serve their favourite sons.

Rhodri was transparent about his campaign funding. £2,000 was a loan from his brother. At least one Welsh MP gave Rhodri the 1% of his salary that some Welsh MPs pay annually to Labour Party Wales. The rest came from rank and file supporters. Even though Rhodri's had clever resourceful staff, his was a penny farthing operation compared with the Alun's lavishly staffed and funded Rolls Royce. Rules had been agreed to ensure that internal Labour election were contested on a fair basis. They were shamelessly and repeatedly violated by Alun's side.

The secrets of Alun's campaign fund were not revealed to journalists who inquired. Peter Hain, his campaign manager, was moonlighting as a Minister in the Welsh Office. Julie Crowley, another government employee and paid by the state, accompanied Alun on a number of engagements, during her 'time off'. Civil servants briefed Alun fo media appearances during the campaign.

A sympathetic union provided Alun with office and telephone Rhodri hired rooms in a Cardiff Arcade. Some volunteers manned both A study of the diaries of civil servants during the campaign wou demonstrate the difficulty in drawing a line between their official duti and serving Alun's internal Party needs. Some civil servants were said have taken leave of absence for the campaign. In the interests of the civ servants themselves clear definitions should be promulgated on the divisions of work. There is story to tell on this that is beyond the scop of this book.

The entire workforce of the Labour Party Wales office in Transpo House in Cardiff appeared to be working as part of Alun' s team. Bu Welsh Office Junior Minister Jon Owen Jones was silent and inactiv during the latter half of the campaign. His and Peter's Ministeri futures were now pre-determined.

Channel Four's 'Dispatches' and the BBC's 'Panorama' produce piercing investigative programmes. George Wright was the star of bot The broadcasters were fascinated with the TGWU's internal machin tions and their innovative concept of democracy. A researcher rang m and said she had money to conduct research into the views of TGW members. 'Where', she asked, 'could we find large groups of them th would be representative of the whole Union?'

Easy in theory. Just hang round outside the factory gate Unfortunately, that method is no longer practical because most worke now drive to work. The TGWU, in the form of George Wright, w unhelpful. With full co-operation from TGWU, a scientifically repre sentative sample of the Union could have been polled. Full guarante were given on confidentiality, but George was not playing.

'Spin Doctor' reported that the Welsh based company Beaufo Research had refused to accept a commission to find out the views TGWU members on Alun and Rhodri. The reason given was the stro likelihood that the Union bosses in Wales would disapprove of such poll.

Dispatches organised their own ballot, employing Cardiff and Bang University students to poll members of the Union. It was conducted consultation with Harris Research and the Electoral Reform Society ensure that it was representative and statistically reliable. 668 membe were interviewed. 471 for Rhodri, 182 for Alun, a 70 : 30 split.

The results were given to George on camera. He was unhappy with having the poll 'sprung' on him by the interviewer. First, he doubted its veracity and then refused to comment further. He became so rattled he mentioned the surprise candidate 'Alun Morgan'.

I know from the TGWU that we're backing the Secretary of State because he's the Secretary of State. Very good logical reasons for doing so. Now we're not here in an anti-Rhodri campaign – he's a member of ours ... he's a friend ... Rhodri has his qualities. Alun Morgan (sic) has equal qualities ... but he's the Secretary of State ... If Rhodri was the Secretary of State for Wales we'd back him.

Naked, unashamed and exposed was the Union's contempt for democracy and their deference to authority figures. Here was an old fashioned Trade Union wheeler-dealer in action. George was equally riveting on Panorama. He was a blend of menace and bluster. At one point, he turned on the interviewer and snapped that he had been han-dling people like him for 20 years.

George could find no plausible reason why he would cast 100% of his Union's votes for Alun while Channel Four's independent poll of TGWU members found they wanted Rhodri – apart from 'George knows best'.

The Observer said that there's a future for George's ballot technique with a retirement job in North Korea. There was a great deal of atten-tion paid throughout the UK to New Labour's loss of innocence. Alun's shabby coalition of patronage and vested interests was stripped bare. It was payroll votes, Blair's acolytes and Union leaders with hopes of gongs and places in the Lords. They combined the worst bullying tactics of Old Labour Trade Union bosses with the power greed of New Labour control-freakery.

Where no Skylarks Sing

THERE was a new spring in Ron's step.

His support for Alun was in spite of Alun's spasmodic record on devolution. He agonised over the decision. He knew Alun's weaknesses and disliked his style. Ron was conscious of the trouble he had already caused the Party and the Prime Minister. He had given a commitment in his letter of resignation to support the new Secretary of State. Did this commit him in the internal party election? Ron was worried that Welsh devolution was too fragile a creature to trust to the care of the mercurial Rhodri. He believed that new tensions would result from Rhodri's reaction to pressures. There were other factors. Resentment at Rhodri's challenge to his Leadership of the Assembly still rankled. It had been a lacerating battle and the wounds had not healed.

My memories of the Ron-Rhodri fight were of a wasted, bitter summer. I was Chair of the Welsh Group of Labour MPs at the time and took an anti-election stance. I told both Ron and Rhodri to their faces that I would publicly support neither of them. Both were well respected close friends. I urged Rhodri to stand down because I was convinced that Ron was certain to win.

It was difficult to tell Rhodri that I thought he had no chance. The politically smart move would have been to tell both candidates that I was backing them. Some did. After all, it was a secret ballot.

Rhodri was a clear winner in the Hustings. Relaxed, humorous and authoritative, he charmed audiences of Party members. Ron was tense, repetitive and charmless. The mood of the Party was to get a quick result to compress internal Party warfare into a period of a few weeks.

Rumours of Ron's alleged 'cruising' activities multiplied in the Gwent area. Several Labour politicians had heard stories about incidents at the Llwyn Hir car park. They never reached my ears, but I did have an invitation to ring a farmer 'friend' in the Newport area 'who had something important to tell me'. I assumed it was another wheeze to persuade me to back moves to stuff more taxpayers' money into farmers' pockets. He was not a constituent and I did not ring back.

The stories did get through to Rhodri's campaign office. Rhodri arranged a meeting with Ron to tell him face to face that the rumours were detailed, frequent and persuasive. Rhodri had been falsely smeared in the past and his sympathies were all with Ron. Rhodri fully accepted Ron's assurance that the stories were malicious 'bullshit'. On no occasion, public or private, did Rhodri ever pass on the stories that continued to arrive every day. I have powerful reasons for believing this.

But Ron was and remains deeply suspicious. A reporter rang Ron' political adviser Huw Roberts during the campaign with tales of the unexpected. Huw dismissed these as malicious gossip invented by the Gwent farming community. A person in Ron's team says that a respected Welsh journalist was approached by a member of Rhodri's team with rumours. Ron was not told of this until after his resignation.

It may be facile to explain Ron's backing for Alun as personal ambition. It was widely believed that they had done a deal. The two had never previously warmed to each other. There was suspected, active animosity between Ron and Alun. In the past there had been a deep friendship between Ron and Rhodri. Ron may have become embittered in his belief that malicious stories had been spread by Rhodri supporters, if not by Rhodri himself. Their relationship was soured by perception that Rhodri had not fought a clean fight. He had.

MPs hunger for the August recess of long empty days when demand on their time are sparse. It's an essential respite from the continuous strain of the helter-skelter of meetings, speeches and decisions. Ron was in despair, the holiday he needed was displaced by an unnecessary month of gruelling campaign.

He now admits that his first decision of not sharing a platform with Rhodri was a mistake. He intended to deny Rhodri the profile and credibility that the Secretary of State already had. This tactic is widely adopted by sitting MPs in fending off their challengers. But in this contest it was seen as a retreat by Ron from debate.

Ron was already overburdened. Win had been sacked and his replacement, Jon Owen Jones, was still finding his feet at a time when the reorganisation of the NHS was being planned.

Ron was dragged around thinly attended General Committee

meetings and forced to defend decisions of government with which he disagreed and of local authorities over which he had no responsibility. In Ystradgynlais he lost the vote, largely because of the decision of a local planning inspector on an open-cast issue. In Bridgend, he was on the receiving end of dissatisfaction at the failure of a local hall to obtain funding and in the Gower he was judged to be at fault for the decision of the Boundary Commission to alter the County boundaries.

Elsewhere he was hounded because of twinning and the location of the Welsh Assembly building. Old warriors of the anti-devolution debate exhumed their malice. 'For the first time in my life', said Ron, 'I am seen as part of the establishment'. Understandably, he may have privately prayed that the heavens would rid him of this turbulent Rhodri.

Rhodri's popularity won him a surprisingly high vote from the constituencies. The final overall result was accepted because Ron won all three sections, democratic and undemocratic. Ron was victorious but exhausted, and very angry with Rhodri. But there may have been reasons other than hubris that persuaded Ron to back Alun in the second campaign.

Ron is an astute political tactician. His life's ambition to lead the Assembly had not been left behind on Clapham Common. Throughout the three months of the Alun and Rhodri campaign, I believe his aim was the Leadership for himself. He always had a high opinion of Rhodri's talents. They worked together to wreck the Cardiff Bay Barrage Act and successfully delayed its progress for many months. Largely because of their obstruction, the Barrage bill was stuck in Parliament for a longer period than the First World War.

When Ron led the Welsh frontbench team in opposition, he let Rhodri have full freedom to 'do his own thing'. He saw him as an unguided but effective missile. But Ron also valued his encyclopaedic memory, the teeming brain that ensured that Rhodri hit more targets than most shadow Ministers. These were dangerous talents in a competitor. Rhodri was likely to be a successful, charismatic First Secretary who would be difficult to remove.

Ron had fought for Rhodri to be a Minister instead of Peter Hain. The announcement of the new government in 1997 was delayed because Ron was still arguing. But, on the Monday following the General Election, he was told he could not have Rhodri. The word from Downing Street was that Ron would have to make his mind up whether or not he wanted to be in the Cabinet. Rhodri and his friends were devastated. Tony Blair's excuse that Rhodri was too old for a junior Minister's job was baffling. The new rule was rumoured to be 'no jobs to anyone over 55 years of age, unless they had an Oscar or two'.

The loyalty Ron owed to Rhodri had died in the first year of the Labour government. He was exasperated by what he saw as Rhodri's sniping over the Cardiff Bay Barrage and City Hall issues.

Ron spoke to Alun several times after his resignation and always said that he would support his campaign. Alun was grateful and thanked Ron for being 'helpful.' Peter Hain encouraged Ron to go forth and campaign in the constituencies. But Alun was vulnerable. He could lose the Leadership, even fail to be elected on the high-risk list in Mid and West Wales. Even if he surmounted those hurdles, there was a further problem, as Ron pointed out on UK national television. The Wales Act provided for the election of the First Secretary to be made by the elected AMs at their first meeting in May. Ron saw that as his best chance.

He kept in close contact with all potential AMs. Candidates were phoned repeatedly. Ron's offer to campaign in all winnable constituencies may have had a dual purpose. He has the useful knack of winning the confidence of political colleagues. It was this gift that had secured his place in Shadow Cabinet elections and won his right, subsequently, to a place in the Cabinet.

That position may have falsely appeared to have flattered his talents. He was not an impressive Commons or media performer. Dogged canvassing of support among colleagues ensured that he often punched above his political weight.

But his talents were not all on display in the front window. He has determination in greater measure than most fellow MPs. His concentration on clear objectives is fixed and persistent. Throughout his career he has proved to be a fine organiser and he successfully delegated tasks to others. His leadership qualities are first rate and he has overcome some mountainous problems.

But his old magic was dulled by the unanswered questions left over from Clapham Common. He won few new friends among the aspirant AMs. Most were irritated by his phonecalls. They recognised his unspoken ambition to displace Alun or Rhodri.

Ron found a useful diversion. Shortly after Clapham Common he began to write a pamphlet on devolution for the Institute of Welsh Affairs. This was a cathartic process for him. There was productive life outside of the Cabinet. The huge 500 strong turn-out for his lecture gave his self-confidence a much needed boost. It was especially gratifying compared with the pitifully tiny congregations on Alun's 'Miss the People' tour. The event was described as a watershed in his 'rehabilitation'; unfortunately it was an audience of the great and good. It gave him a false impression of the level of support for him within the Labour Party.

At an earlier event at the Park Hotel, his former Permanent Secretary Rachel Lomax, in an unprecedented public move by a distinguished civil servant, publicly embraced him. A queue formed to shake his hand. It was his first public appearance post-Clapham and it was a triumph.

Ron was half-way to convincing the people of Wales that he had been victimised. The sleaze fixated London media was blamed for the downfall. Peter Dobbie in the Daily Mail spoke up for sleaze.

Surely in the valleys, a place where men do not normally dance at both ends of the ballroom or take leafy rambles with newly-met males, they would torch Ron if he tried to butter them up?

Ron also fulfilled another long-standing engagement, to address a meeting devoted to the joys of nature. It was the launch of the Royal Society for the Protection of Birds manifesto on the Assembly. It was an orchestrated part of Ron's 'rehabilitation' by his friends. Ron never used the word 'rehabilitation' because he did not think he had done anything wrong. On view at the Park Hotel Cardiff on the 22nd of January was a glimpse of the old Ron. He delights in the natural world and is especially knowledgeable about birdlife. That was the root of his anger and opposition to the Cardiff Bay which will drown mudscapes that are habitats of thousands of birds.

Lamenting the decline in several bird species, including the lapwing, chough and black grouse, he asked: 'Few tears would be shed perhaps at the decline of the common house sparrow, but do we really want to hand over to our children a Wales where no skylarks sing?'

The next time he mentioned his bird watching activities, he was not believed.

The Union of Fixers and Riggers

'L'appetit vient en mangeant'—*The appetite grows by eating*
Rabelais

RHODRI'S campaign troughed with the Engineers Union vote.

His entanglement with a train door and the consequent prominent black eye demoralised him. The disarming, casual speech he used to warm-up audiences left the largely hostile AEEU delegates cold. Alun's speech was better organised but as somnolent as ever. The delegates had been under heavy pressure to back Alun from their own leaders.

The system used by the AEEU and, later, by the GMB, had much in common with the parodies of democracy practised by Ceaucescu and Stalin, embryonically democratic but far removed from Omov. Perhaps, in future Labour Party elections, we could invite international observers from the UN to check the validity of our caricature of democracy?

220 delegates were entitled to vote. 72 did, 42 for Alun and 28 for Rhodri. Some delegates had balloted their members: others had not. Under AEEU rules, the votes of all 65,000 of its members were cast for Alun.

One hack has a diverting tale about the audience reaction to Alun's speech. He had been introduced for the first time to Daily Telegraph columnist Sion Simon just before Alun spoke. The hack writes:

I was most surprised when after Alun's address Simon warmly applauded. I assumed he was there as a journalist. In more than 20 years as a journalist I have never seen a working journalist applauding a politician. It just isn't done. It was only later that I learnt that Simon had at one time worked at Millbank and he harbours an ambition to become MP for the Rhondda.

Rhodri was at home in the Swansea area, where his family have their roots. After a Hustings meeting in the city, he legged it to the local Pen and Wig to explain to the drinkers there that the contest was about to be made into BBC soap opera named 'BlairykissAlun'. Occasionally breaking into Welsh, Rhodri devoured his burger and convinced the Swansea Jacks he was one of them. Alun was whisked back to London in his chauffeured car, his nose deep into his red boxes.

With incurable sycophancy, Alun's team attributed the AEEU result to Blair's second visit to Wales the previous day. He had a question and answer session with Party members at the other end of Wales in Theatr Clwyd in Mold, North Wales. It had been another dose of his worn out mind-numbing spiel, with one unscripted moment. Blair underlined his preference for Alun when the Welsh Secretary prompted him in one answer. 'See what a good job he does', Tony told the audience. It's odd that such commonplace remarks are classed as 'witty' when said by a Prime Minister or a Consort to a Monarch. But it was the most thrilling thing he had said all day.

John Marek, MP and Assembly candidate for Wrexham, had put Blair on the defensive in North Wales. The Daily Post led with John's attack on Blair's electioneering trip. Rhodri's camp were relaxed. They knew Tony's halo had lost its radiance in Wales. The disappointments with New Labour were profound. Downing Street was buttressing a campaign that was crumbling. Alun's camp was in a state of of perpetual anxiety.

Worry turned to panic when a major telephone poll for the Western Mail and Wales on Sunday produced a result of 6,117 votes for Rhodri to 599 for Alun, 9-1 in Rhodri's favour. Telephone polls are rightly derided because they are universally manipulated. This time, precautions had been taken to outlaw multiple voting.

Alun dismissed the poll as a 'crude and meaningless form of entertainment'. Alun's groupie Don Touhig, flaunting his impressive command of the obvious, revealed that 'the real poll will be of Party members on February 20th'. If only that were true. Campaign choreographer Hain was more imaginative. 'We've had reports from all over Wales saying Plaid Cymru and the Tories have been voting for Rhodri in an attempt to cause chaos' he fantasised.

Without the benefits of 'reports from all over Wales', Rhodri divined that 'Alun Michael's strategy of playing it long has rebounded'.

George Wright had not attempted to achieve even the North Korean mockery of democracy. In his case, it was not one member: one vote but one member: 53,000 votes. They were all added to Alun's swelling 'rotten boroughs' pile from the 'Fixers and Riggers' Unions.

My own Union GPMU were impossible to pin down. I wrote to Welsh Executive member and GPMU Union official Garry Owen calling for a democratic vote. The answer was almost incomprehensible but conveyed a negative message. I was unaware that the writer had been mentioned in previous allegations of vote rigging in an internal ballot. In December it was reported by Wales on Sunday that Garry Owen had sent a circular telling members not to return ballot papers directly to the company running the election. Instead, they should hand their voting slips to branch officials who would send them on in bulk. Garry Owen was not disciplined because he was not thought to be at fault but, as mentioned, earlier, another official was. Wales on Sunday reported on January 26th:

This coming Sunday, Garry Owen will be seeking selection as Labour Assembly candidate for Pontypridd. I am confident that the ballot will be conducted without criticism, unlike the print Union vote Garry was involved in last summer. Garry, deputy branch secretary of the GPMU Union, was criticised by independent scrutineers for interfering improperly in the ballot, which had to be re-run.

Like tens of thousands of other Union members in Wales, I never had a chance to use my Trade Union vote. My wife wrote to George Wright demanding her say as a TGWU member. George's reply was as helpful as Garry Owen's. With some satisfaction, I heard that the immaculately democratic and very able Jane Davidson won the nomination and is now AM for Pontypridd.

An old friend who has spent a lifetime as a branch official in the steel Union ISTC contacted me following the web publication of this book. We had laboured together in the steel plant at Llanwern for decades. He too had no Union vote. After exhaustive inquiries he had traced the only record of the ISTC vote, buried in pygmy print on page 195 of a quarterly report:

With the General Secretary now in the House of Lords, the Confederation (ISTC) will have political representation at all levels. With regard to the election of Leader of the Welsh Assembly, it had been decided to support Mr Alun Michael MP.

'Who decided?' my friend asked, 'And is there any significance in the juxtaposition of these two sentences?'

DID THEY SQUEAK?

'In politics what begins in fear ends in folly'

Coleridge.

THE DREAD of defeat infected the inner core of Alun's supporters. They were, mostly, fiercely careerist politicians who yearn to hold and retain high office. It's an uncomfortable life that always ends in disappointment and failure.

Apprehension incited the folly of a plea for a third visit from Blair. Morgan supporter John Marek again attacked Blair's further excursion on February 2nd as 'a panic reaction'. 'The Prime Minister', he said, 'should stop and think and say to himself, should he go on fighting the people's wishes or should he accept them'.

This visit was timed to influence the ballot of Party members. It was arranged for the day ballot papers went out to the 25,000 members in Wales for the Omov ballot of the grassroots section of the electoral college. The itinerary was bizarre. Two sites were favoured. One, a visit to a computer facility at Duffryn School in my constituency, the other to a nursing school in the Cardiff North constituency of Julie Morgan, Rhodri's wife. Was this planned as a strike at the heart of enemy territory?

In Newport, he was 'impressed by the computers'. Unfortunately, the Prime Minister's judgment in this area is not greatly valued. It was wickedly said that, after he tried to correct his spelling mistakes on the family computer at Number 10, Cherie Blair had to remove the Tippex from the monitor screen.

Later that day, he may have wished to Tippex out his stern advice to Labour members. 'Don't think, 'wouldn't it be a nice idea to give Tony Blair a bloody nose?" To thousands, that was a temptation too delicious to resist.

While the rank and file were preparing to vote, there was strong confirmation of Rhodri's overwhelming popularity. Quality democracy was about to rear its unfamiliar head. There had been eager anticipation of the first large scale Omov ballot, of UNISON members. Victory for Alun would have bolstered his claim that it was not only Rhodri who had rank-and-file support. It would also guarantee him a majority in the Trade Union section of the three-part electoral college.

The Omov ballot of UNISON's 50,000 members triumphantly backed Rhodri, by three to one. Peter Hain, who was branding himself as a bottom feeder in the electoral pond, dredged up this sour excuse: 'This was more a vote for apathy than for Rhodri. It is a small vote in the big election which Alun is still on course to win'.

The man who had been called Rhodri's George Stephanopoulos, Kevin Brennan, tartly snapped back:

The turnout was very much in line with that when Tony Blair was elected Labour Leader. It was certainly good enough then, and that was for the leadership of the Labour Party as a whole. It's the largest vote by far in this election. It's certainly better to have 19% of members voting than 19 officials deciding in a room.

Peter Hain had not finished. He reached the nadir of his campaigning career with a jibe about Trotskyists in UNISON. It was as crude and dishonourable as any Cold War 'Reds under the Bed' scare. It is meaningless in today's politics, but a desperate campaigner says desperate things.

Now, he is ashamed of it because it has tarnished his good name. Later, he tried to erase it from his and our memories. At the time, he was so proud of it that he repeated it in the Dispatches programme in what looked like a staged conversation with Terry Thomas. He said:

The problem is you've got quite a lot of people who are active in UNISON in particular who are not in the Labour Party but who want to defeat Alun to create problems for the Labour government don't they? So there's like, you know, Trotskyists and others who have got no time for the Labour Party.

There were other worrying signs that New Labour as an organism was suffering from some form of mental illness. A spokesperson in London said that 'In a city of 6 million, it's sad if you can muster only 1,000 for a rally'. Only 1,000! He was badmouthing one of the largest political meetings for years, held in support of Ken Livingstone.

Mark Steel in the Guardian diagnosed the problem. On Peter Hain's analysis of the vote, he was saying that there were about 5,000 Trotskyists in UNISON in Wales. Should you expect a park-keeper in Cardiff to say at closing time:

Time soon for the mighty roar of the downtrodden masses in their just historic proletarian battle, in it? If Hain mentioned his theory to his doctor, the GP would say, 'Yeees, that's right Peter. Trotskyists? Thousands of them aren't there? Are they here now? Do they come at night and talk in squeaky voices inside your head?

A STITCH IN TIME

'A oes heddiw am swyddau megis hyn yn ymgashau? Ni chredir yn wir i neb ond i un a Dauwyneb'—Today, merely for the sake of office do people hate each other like this? No one is now believed unless he is two faced'

Tudur Aled, XVI century.

LESS THAN a fortnight away from the result, tension was high. Neither candidate had a clear lead.

Leaving no fix unfixed, the Party set about stitching up another sector of the electoral college. This was subtle and complex, requiring the full might of the Party machine to execute. It finally killed any lingering notion that the Labour Party apparatchiks were impartial.

The angriest exchanges between the two sides were sparked off by the selection of the list candidates. The choice was vital because it was Alun's only chance of becoming a member of the Assembly. He had to be placed in the best position of all the 20 candidates.

The system adopted was that the 40 seats, corresponding to Westminster constituencies, would be decided by a first past the post result in the traditional way. The other twenty AMs would be 'elected' by proportional representation. It was a novel procedure and was little understood- even in Wales. Electors had two votes. One for named candidate in the first past the post Assembly seat. The second was a party. The votes of losing parties would be added in each Euro-constituency. The extra Assembly seats would be distributed on the basis of total votes achieved by parties whose candidates did not win in the first past the post constituencies.

Even at this stage, it was thought that Labour would secure very few list AMs. Two were optimistically predicted. Labour's forecasted dominance in the first-past-the-post seats would result in consolation list seats for the other parties who were expected to come second or third in many seats.

But there was a vital new imperative in elbowing Alun's candidates into the list places. All 20 candidates selected would have a vote in the leadership election with the equivalent weight of a vote of an MP or an MEP. Each individual list candidate had the voting strength of 300 individual Party members. The 20 picked could nullify the votes of a quarter of the total Welsh membership. A predominance of candidates for Alun or Rhodri in the lists could swing the final victory.

The original, idealistic advocates of PR believed that the top-up list seats should go to the best losers in the first past the post election. The system adopted by Labour gave unprecedented power to the Party machine. The on-message and fully lobotomised could be crow barred onto the lists, even though they have not won, or even sought, the approval of Party members in the constituencies. This was an entirely new and audacious form of patronage.

The Western Mail described the selection process as 'civil war'. This was the final battle that would decide the result of the entire conflict. There was another delicious twist. The panel that made the final decision on the list included a place for the Secretary of State. Instead of the electorate choosing the candidate, this could have been one of the rare examples in Western Europe of a candidate choosing the electorate. Alun declined the temptation to select himself, possibly as one stitch-up too far.

Alun's caucus was alarmed by the arithmetic. Their calculation for the three sections of the electoral college was that Alun was overwhelmingly ahead with the Trade Unions, a majority of Party members were going for Rhodri, but that the third section, of MPs / MEPs / Assembly Candidates, was a headache.

Alun's team were working on assumptions of: 21 MPs for Alun, 13 for Rhodri; 3 MEPs for Alun, 2 for Rhodri; and 10 Assembly candidate for Alun, 30 for Rhodri. Rhodri's team had a different forecast. They were counting on 10 MPs, 2 MEPs, plus a large majority of selected Assembly candidates. The only guide to MPs' opinion was a vote in the Welsh Group of MPs. It had divided 11 against and 10 for Omov in the Trade Union sector for the Alun-Rhodri election.

Within the space of a few months, Welsh MPs had voted overwhelmingly for Omov in the Ron-Rhodri election and against Omov in the Alun-Rhodri one. The earth had moved in Westminster with a seismic shift of principles, deftly illustrating the 10th precept of Pompomism: 'Select the desired outcome and adjust your principles to achieve it'.

The change between the elections was profound and explains the wide variations from the two camps in the votes anticipated from MPs. Could this possibly mean that MPs do not always tell the truth?

Alun's camp had a new fear to keep them awake at night. If Rhodri supporters were a majority in the 20 candidates in the list seats, it could result in the horror of Rhodri winning in two sectors and Alun winning only one. He would obviously owe his victory to the Old Labour cart horses of the Trade Unions. The loop ordered stitch-up number seven. It was delivered.

In normal times, the process would have been a good natured piece of wheeler-dealing to find places for everyone's favourites. Now, the Assembly Leadership was at stake, the future direction of politics in Wales was in the balance. More importantly, the declared will of Tony Blair could be defied. Rhodri's team was also preoccupied with the lists. One of them quotes 'a campaigner of distinction and success since the sixties' who said 'Alun cannot be allowed to lose'.

This was no longer merely trench warfare, it was hand to hand fighting – in one case, possibly literally so. All Assembly panel candidates who had failed to secure a constituency were told they could apply to be added to the list.

They were interviewed. Some proved to be very strong candidates, others distressingly weak. A London official of the Party and Terry Thomas then produced their model recommended candidates list. It bore no resemblance to the performances of the hopefuls; so blatantly unfair were they to Rhodri's supporters, that uproar resulted. The favoured lists were stuffed with Michael fans. Terry Thomas was, of course, a fully engaged pro-Alun campaigner. He had been filmed ridiculing the prospect of Wales dominated by Rhodri and Rod Richards, 'a country', he warned, 'without a single statesman'.

Some of the grassroots delegates from the constituencies objected to Terry's key role. Their protests were brushed aside. The delegates were told there could be no changes. The choice was to accept or reject the list. In a four hour brawl, they voted and rejected the list for Mid and West Wales four times.

The fury was not confined to one region. The lists for South Wales Central and South Wales East were rejected by the constituency delegates. There are delicious anecdotes of the rows within these groups and heroic resistance by constituency delegates against the imposition of Alun's fans.

Rhodri's supporters claimed the Alun's camp had engineered backing for their candidates. There was no doubt of that. Representatives of the rank and file members were in nose to nose confrontation with servants of the Party's centralised control-freaks.

What stirred the wrath even more was the insistence by Alun's persuaders that candidates who had not attempted to win constituency seats were competing for list placings. This was a new back-door entry into the Assembly lubricated by the patronage of the party establishment. Seeking constituency nominations is a gruelling, morale sapping nightmare. But that's been the testing rite of passage undergone by all Labour politicians in the quest to become professionals. Now candidates, who did not bother to undergo that purgatory had their passport to paradise handed over because they backed the establishment candidate. Another new fiddle.

It is not possible to give precise figures of the advantages of the final choice for each candidate. There is a complicating factor because two of the candidates are believed to have changed their allegiances at the last moment. Two names have been quoted by both sides. Not surprisingly, their list was approved without argument as both Alun's and Rhodri's supporters thought they were voting for their own trusted candidates. There remains a simmering sense of betrayal. The developing careers of the universally popular candidates are being watched with keen interest.

In other regions, the constituency representatives remain angry. Dictatorial bullying had displaced reasoned decision making. The seeds of the coming revolt by the faithful were being nourished.

One disturbing and unwelcome side issue was a racial argument. The sincere efforts to field candidates from the minority ethnic communities in Wales had almost entirely failed. The establishment team argued in favour of a high position on the list for Vaughn Gethin, but against high position for Cherry Short, the candidate for Monmouthshire. She was fighting, and nearly won, a marginal seat, and justified a high place. The crucial difference between these two members of ethnic minorities was that Vaughn Gethin was an Alun supporter and Cherry Short backed Rhodri.

The temperature went up several degrees. Peter Hain vehemently denied that the rejection of the Mid and West Wales list with Alun's name on was an embarrassment. 'It's disappointing', he waspishly added, 'there is a factional dispute and an attempt to bump out of the picture an outstanding young Welshman from an ethnic minority'. He did not mention the insistence of his side on bumping out an outstanding young Welshwoman from an ethnic minority.

Indeed, Alun was not the problem, Hain correctly said:

I'm delighted as there was unanimous agreement on the selection Council that Alun should top the list. The fact he opted to stand for the region is a marvellous boost for Mid and West Wales.

The decisions, many taken under duress, went to the Wales Executive to be ratified. It has been calculated that the stitch-up of the list gave Alun 10 additional valuable weighted votes. The Executive was dominated by Michael's backers. Kevin Morgan called them 'Blair's outriders'. They always jumped through hoops when Tony Blair demanded. The Welsh Executive rubberstamped the rigged lists without changes, as they previously rubberstamped the fixed panel and the election process that favoured Alun.

The National Executive in London obediently added their imprimatur. Alun was now in pole position, with the best chance of winning a proportional representation assisted places seat.

For unknown reasons, Peter Hain chose this very moment to fan the flames.

Rhodri's camp has screamed 'foul' from the very beginning. Its position seems to be that if Rhodri does not win something, it's a stitch-up. I think that is a disreputable way to undertake an election.

An un-named spokesperson for the Rhodri camp said that, as the date of the election drew nearer, it could only get bitter. 'It won't be blood on the carpet', they forecast, 'it will be guts on the carpet. It's going to get very nasty'.

The announcement of the final result was just a week away. There was no chance now that it would be accepted as fair by the mass of Party members. The electoral college had only one democratic section - the votes from Party members. Rhodri was certain to win that well and be the moral victor. If Alun claimed victory on the basis of majorities in the two fiddled Union and MPs / MEPs / candidates sections, he would be a Leader with very little credibility.

Labour's General Secretary in Wales, Anita Gale, said forlornly 'my hope is that everyone will unite around the new Leader as we must have unity in the Party'. Some hope.

Many Labour Party supporters, and possibly members, were privately plotting to ventilate their fury on May 6th.

Scourge the Messenger

'If all you have is a hammer, everything begins to look like a nail'
Friedrich Nietzsche

ALUN'S TEAM was rattled by the encouragement for Rhodri from the Western Mail and Wales on Sunday. The Daily Mirror and the People were slavishly pro-Alun and timed their Millbank-inspired praise of him to coincide with key votes in the contest. Many of their editorials sounded as though they have been dictated by Alastair Campbell.

There was no love lost between Rhodri and Alastair. Rhodri won his Spectator award as 'Parliamentary Inquisitor of the Year' for his forensic questioning of Alastair. The Mirror was changing to the 'Welsh Mirror' at this time. Their circulation of about 200,000 copies in Wales is almost four times that of the Western Mail. The typical Western Mail reader is a 55 year old Welsh speaking farmer from Carmarthen. The Welsh Mirror type is a 45 year old redundant steelworker from Splott. The Mirror's influence on Labour members was at least ten times that of the Western Mail. The timing of the Mirror's blockbusting 'Alun's the Best Man' edition was the 29th of January. Unknown to Rhodri, the date for ending out members' ballot forms had been brought forward.

That weekend, teams of telephone canvassers had been arranged by Alun's team and the Mirror used their frontpage and editorial to boost him. Through no fault of their own, Rhodri's team were caught napping. The charge of collusion from Kevin Brennan is almost certainly justified. Another ploy to be added to the ballot-riggers' manual.

The Mirror political correspondent, Nigel Morris, absolved himself of any accusation of being even-handed in his hagiography of Alun. Rhodri had a single passing mention. Nigel's piece was encrusted with golden quotations of mind-numbing banality from Alun, crafted by the Millbank wordsmiths.

In case the steelworker from Splott was not getting the message, that day's Mirror leader thundered, 'Alun Michael will make sure that thing get done'. The argument was one that played on the perceived weak nesses of Rhodri:

What sort of an Assembly do you think Wales should have? Shoul it be simply a talking shop? Or should it be a proper working bod which tackles the problems of the Welsh people?

The Mirror believes that on that basis there is only one answer – on man who will lead a business-like Assembly. And that is ALUN MICHAEL.

That is, Alun does not speak as well as Rhodri, so if you want to avoi a 'talking shop' you must select the poorest speaker.

Instead of purring with gratitude at the Mirror's support for hir Alun was preoccupied by criticism from papers with far less influenc over voting Labour members. 'The Western Mail and Wales on Sunday said Alun, 'have become participants in this race in a way that I find mo odd and not very objective for newspapers'. Peter Hain was equall resentful, suggesting that 'we had to appeal over the heads of the di being created by this caricature of Alun being seen as London' s man.

A monotone din was heard from the direction of Westminste Virtually identical letters from MPs to Party members were another wa of shooting the messenger. The letters were signed by Clwyd South M Martyn Jones, Pontypridd MP Kim Howells, Clwyd West MP Garet Thomas and Carmarthen West and Pembrokeshire South MP Nic Ainger. The Western Mail claimed that similar letters were also sent ou in Islwyn, Ogmore, Torfaen, Newport East and Neath.

It was all very predictable stuff that was hardly worth the expense a stamp. The letters extolled the virtues of Alun and set out his visio for Wales in the next century, with a thriving economy and first cla public services. His Ministerial experience and current role as Secretar of State were lauded, making Alun 'the natural choice to continue t lead Wales in the Assembly, so we can have a smooth transition of pow from London to Cardiff'.

There was a small variation in Alun's epistle to his own flock. H returned to scourging the media:

You must make up your own mind but in doing so I urge you not let the media dictate the outcome. Some in the media are not so muc reporting the contest but seeking to control the result. We all kno those newspapers have never been the friends of Labour.

No newspapers were mentioned by name, but all the letters had the battle cry 'We must reclaim the election from the journalists!' Sending out the letters was a flagrant abuse of the agreed rules. But, on top of all the other shameless fiddles, it was of little consequence.

The national press were generally in favour of Rhodri as a permanent fountain of sparkling copy. Welsh television channels maintained impartiality. There was unprecedented public fascination with the contest. More of the general public were more excited at the prospect of voting for Alun or Rhodri than they were about voting in the assembly elections. It was a bitter disappointment to many when they discovered that the vote was confined to party members.

In North Wales, the mood of the election was less frenetic. The Daily Post was either neutral or uninterested. Most North Walians are tuned into electronic media from sources outside Wales. The contest was a relatively minor political episode there.

The Western Mail gave equal space to both camps to present the virtues of their icons. Formerly allies in the 'Yes for Wales' campaign, lobbyist Leighton Andrews and Professor Kevin Morgan were now divided in their choices.

Kevin Morgan listed the variety of Rhodri's experience in all-Wales jobs. Trying to impose Alun without a vote proved that 'the patronage state is alive' in Wales. 'Devolution is worthless', he suggested, 'if it doesn't allow us to make our choice of leader without fear, favour and pressure from London'.

Reflecting an opinion poll result which reported that Rhodri would swell Labour's vote by 9%, Kevin argued that 'Rhodri has the capacity to enthuse and mobilise the Labour Party and the wider electorate'.

Leighton Andrews's curious article tried to smother the campaign with a layer of induced boredom. Rhodri was accused of the sin of originality for his one legged duck joke. Leighton displayed his own genius as a trailblazingly original wordsmith by climaxing his praise of Alun with 'Nobody does it better'.

Two media folk in Millbank regularly wager bets on how long certain politicians can go in an interview without uttering their favourite words. Could Ron Davies manage three sentences without an 'inclusive'? With Alun, the bets were on 'partnership' or 'voluntary sector'. It's a contagious trait. Echoing his master's voice, Leighton managed a 'partnership' in the third paragraph.

But the indelible impressions were the visual ones: Western Mail cartoonist Mumph's portrayal of Alun with parachute; Blair's long nose that Wales on Sunday told him to keep out of Wales; plus the universal Rhodri the dragon and Alun the poodle.

STALINIST STITCH

'Diplomacy is saying 'Nice Doggie' until you find a rock'
                                                    Wyn Caitlin

THE FINAL WEEK was not one of heart stopping excitement. It was a predictable slow motion tragedy, moving to the inevitable. The main players reverted to character and overplayed their allotted roles.

Hours after the debacle of Black Wednesday, which would have sent ordinary mortals seeking a hole in which to bury themselves, John Major gave a television interview. He was self assured, unapologetic and demurely trashed his own words uttered four days earlier. Now, on the BBC's 'On the Record' programme, Alun displayed the same, remarkable ability of politicians to air-brush from memory every trace of recent events.

That HTV poll saying Labour's vote in the Assembly Elections would be 9% higher if Rhodri was elected Leader dominated discussion. Our screens showed Alun insisting that he would win a majority in the members section of the electoral college.

By the nightmare standards of the Paxman interview, this was a good performance by Alun. He was relaxed, smiling and made a reasonable best of the preposterous nonsense he was spouting. The whole week was characterised by optimism from Alun's camp. Did they know something?

Alun had reason to be pleased. The penultimate stitch-up had worked. On the Saturday, the finalised list candidates were announced.

The lists for North Wales and South Wales West were not disputed. The Downing Street Politburo of Central Planning pre-determined the list. Very few changes were allowed in the bitterly argued list for the other three seats. Alun's vote had again been inflated by coercion.

But the row was to be proved futile in electoral terms. Later events confirmed that the acrimony had not increased Alun's tally of Assembly groupies, apart from himself. Gareth Hughes, a rejected candidate and close ally of Ron Davies, accused the Party of using the tactics of an 'old Stalinist regime'.

The final list was:

South Wales Central	Rhodri Morgan
	Sue Essex
	Ken Hopkins
	Wendy Morgan.
South Wales East	Angie Ash
	Brian Smith
	Cherry Short
	Miqdad Al Nuami.
South Wales West	Mair Francis
	Hywel Francis
	Robert Smith
	Paul Griffiths.
Mid and West Wales	Alun Michael
	Delyth Evans
	Vaughan Gethin
	Sioned Mair Richards.
North Wales	Tom Jones
	Margaret Pritchard
	Eifion Williams
	Nia Roberts.

Alun also put 'On The Record' his view that it was essential for whoever won the contest to have the support of the Party's mass membership. He put the boot into democracy, claiming the the UNISON Omov vote was 'less testing' that the AEEU delegate vote. In a total shutdown of his brain by amnesia, he recalled that 'all the back-biting the leadership contest had come from the Morgan camp'.

On the same programme, Rhodri prophetically warned that 'we must come out of this smelling of roses. We need a leadership that's totally credible on the doorsteps and in the election campaign and totally proof against attacks from other parties'.

It was the stench of outrage that TGWU shop steward Colin Adams detected. On the TGWU vote for Alun, he spoke for three quarters of the Union's members. 'We are very upset about the way the decision has been made by a small number of people at the higher level of the Union', he said, 'whereas the grassroots would support Rhodri Morgan'.

When pressed, some of Alun's memory cells were activated. Still insisting on the immaculate conduct of his team, Alun did confess that Peter Hain had been 'forced to respond to some of the whispering and background activities that have gone on'. But when it was put to him that damage had been done to the Labour Party in Wales, he said, 'Oh yes, but I don't put the blame on Peter or those who supported me'. Of course not.

Was Peter privy to the secret knowledge that suffused the whole Alun team in anticipatory bliss? Peter's radiant self-confidence beamed through his permanent sun-tan. His campaigning record was miraculous. The scintillating triumph of the 'Stop the '70 Tour' against apartheid was initiated by him in 1969, just after he started wearing long pants.

He had managed all-Welsh campaigns too. The glorious sequence was: General Election ('epoch-making'); and devolution 'Yes' vote ('historic reverse of '79'). He was not the campaign manger who had delivered Ron's Assembly Leadership victory in all three sections, but he had been influential in shaping the strategy of Angharad Davies. For most of that election he was off on a trade mission to South Africa and Ron had not asked him to do the job.

Peter was rightly proud of his work in the Referendum campaign and the huge vote he helped to deliver in Neath. He could rightly claim that devolution would not have been secured without his campaigning skills. Now, he was supremely confident of an Alun victory, 'but not by a mile' he warned. But his euphoria was still intact. He told the Western Mail, in words that he would later eat, 'no-one doubts there will be anything but a Labour victory on May 6'.

Kevin Brennan's crystal ball was also defective. 'I still believe Labour will perform very strongly in the Assembly elections', he said, 'but : Rhodri won the leadership, we would win them emphatically'.

The result of the ballot was to be announced at 11am on Saturday February 20th at the newly built five-star St David's Hotel in Cardi Bay. In the hope of establishing themselves as king-maker, the GMB ha delayed announcing their result to the final moment. Possibly, ther were other motives. They had at their command a winning 6.2% of th vote.

Kevin Brennan said that his calculations were based on the GMI backing Alun. 'We are heading for a photo-finish'. To win, Rhodr would need 76% in the first section of the electoral college, the Om ballot of all 25,000 members of the Labour Party in Wales.

Kevin consoled himself that this was possible. The UNISON Om ballot, opinion polls from NOP, and the Dispatches television pro gramme had given Rhodri 74%, 75% and 72% support respectively.

There had been teasing speculation of a third solution that coul reverse the effect of a victory by either candidate. The Alun-Rhodr scrap was universally described as the election of the Leader of th Assembly. But the Wales Act had stipulated that the Leader of th Assembly would be the choice of Assembly Members. They would n be elected until May 6th and political control by Labour was not cer tain.

So, a victory by Alun could be overturned by a majority of AM Peter Hain said he was '300% certain' that this would not happen. Kevi Brennan agreed. 'There's no question of anyone not accepting th result', he said, 'on the assumption, of course, there's no ballot-riggin The result will be accepted with dignity, win, lose or draw'. Kevin co cluded with the inevitable sporting analogy. 'If it's a draw, there'll be run-off marathon'. In the last marathon in which both men took par Rhodri beat Alun by an hour.

The GMB continued to taunt, or were they playing a different gam They said the branches' 'consultation' had been completed, independ ently verified and endorsed by its Political Committee and Sout Western Regional Committee.

'The Union will now be informing our branches by post the resu of their ballot', their statement continued. 'There will be no other off cial statement to the media until Friday, February 19 at 11am'. That w 24 hours before the declaration of the overall result.

On the basis of known votes by big GMB branches, Rhodri was optimistic. But caution warned him that the GMB had close ties with Alun, and with Terry Thomas. Alun was a GMB sponsored MP. Terry Thomas is a retired official of the Union. Alun's election agent is a GMB official involved in representing workers in local authorities, including many in Direct Labour Organisations.

The GMB's election process was and remains a mystery. Details of the votes remained under lock and key even after the result was announced. A member of GMB wrote to me two months later alleging ballot rigging. A student researcher sought details later. I also wrote to them while preparing this book. Both requests went unanswered.

Wales on Sunday received a letter from a GMB member alleging skullduggery'. They requested a breakdown of the branch votes. Innocently, the letter asked 'How do you account for the fact that your consultation results are wholly out of kilter with every Omov ballot that has taken place?' The letter asked serious questions and contained challenging figures.

The reply received was waffle. Their regional political officer John Frank disregarded the questions and blandly replied 'The ballot was carried out in accordance with the GMB rules'. To this day, there has been no revelation of how they arrived at their decision. Yet it decided the result. Why the continuing secrecy?

A question mark will permanently hang over the good name of the GMB until they open their results to public scrutiny. To nobody's surprise, this farce ended with Alun receiving all of the GMB's 6.2% share of the total vote. It was more than enough to give Alun his 5% victory. It put a pool of brown foul water between the two candidates. This was the penultimate enigma. From a democratic view it was the penultimate stitch-up.

Another drama involving the same players was running parallel to the battle over the GMB vote.

In his job as Secretary of State for Wales, Alun had the tricky task of clamping down on the inefficient Direct Labour Organisations (DLOs) of many Councils in Wales. Some of them were crying out for government intervention. They were alleged to be scandalously wasteful.

Cardiff's had been running a loss of £2 million per year, Rhondda Cynon Taff's (RCT) was a basket case. Some Councils, including Cardiff and the Vale of Glamorgan took successful action to get their

DLOs in order. RCT did not. Even after many warnings and face-t
face dressing-downs from Secretary of State Alun Michael, RCT co
tinued to accumulate losses. In England, the equivalent Minister, Hila
Armstrong, had acted firmly against similar Councils who were as rec
citrant as RCT. To end huge losses, the English Councils' DLO wo
had been put out to tender. Those were tough but correct decisions.

Action was long overdue against the half a dozen wasteful Counc
in Wales. This is archetypical New Labour policy, to fearlessly take
Old Labour-run, inefficient local Councils. But there was a giant pol
ical dimension.

Enforcing open tendering would result in the loss of thousands
jobs, mostly those of GMB members. The worst offenders were
Labour controlled Councils and three sets of elections were immine
Some argued that by acting tough against unpopular local Counc
Alun would have gained electoral support for Labour. Some said othe
wise.

There is no certain answer on whether Alun's intervention wou
have been politically beneficial or not. But the subsequent electi
results suggest that acting against the DLOs might have avoided t
haemorrhage of Labour votes in the Rhondda, Cynon Valley a
Pontypridd.

Whatever the pressures, the decision was taken not to force the DL(
out to tender. Hundreds of GMB jobs were saved, at least for a whi
The problems in RCT continues now that Plaid is in control. Acti
was inevitable. The possible loss of jobs may have increased because
the delay. RCT now have a loss of £5.3m.

It is not always appreciated that politicians have to strictly compar
mentalise issues. Otherwise, conflicts of interests might occur. Alu
brain had three distinct decisions to be taken simultaneously.

In compartment one of his brain was the need to impose long ove
due financial discipline on badly run Councils. But that could be do
only at the price of antagonising the GMB. He had been a loyal frie
of the GMB.

In compartment two he was worried about possible defeat a
humiliation if he lost the vote against Rhodri. The GMB had a dec
sive 6.2% of the vote and an unexaminable, unaccountable and impe
etrable voting system that could have given their block votes to eith
candidate.

In compartment three was the anxiety about gaining a majority in the Assembly elections. Certain Labour Councils were unpopular. Would the voters punish Assembly candidates unless Alun acted? Or would action by him be judged as the Welsh Office victimising impoverished areas? The retribution of the voters could come from another direction.

Certainly, a person of the calibre of Alun Michael would not allow the separate issues to overlap in any way. The bitter irony is that Alun, the shining New Labour apostle, was wrestling with the problem of over-manning with Old Labour Trade Unions Barons at the same moment as the Barons were determining the future leadership of Wales with Old Labour block votes, while simultaneously trying to maintain Old Labour over-manning with Old Labour Councils. It's a surprise that Alun's brain receptors did not short circuit and implode.

Last minute television interviews by Don Touhig and Peter Hain flowed with the assurance of victory. One TV reporter assured me that he had been told by an Alun aide on the Friday night that a 5% Michael victory was in the bag. There was one theme only, to shut the mouths of anyone who might criticise the fixes after the result was announced. 'Woe betide anyone', warned Don Touhig, 'who questions the result on Saturday'.

It's comfortable to say that, when you know what the result will be.

Nightmare on Cardiff Bay

'New Jerusalem cannot be built on top of a dung hill'
Old Testament Prophets (at Amigos').

IT LOOKS LIKE a giant, grounded bird, one wing half-raised, ready to soar aloft again.

The St David's Hotel and Spa is a wondrous sight to those of us who grew up near what is now called Cardiff Bay. The Docks and Marl areas were long despised and shunned by Cardiffians. Their renaissance fractured Alun and Rhodri's friendship. The Cardiff Bay Barrage bills spanned three Parliaments and poisoned relations among Welsh MPs, between valley and town, and between East and West Wales.

The row with Alun (pro-barrage) and Rhodri (anti-barrage) created an unbridgeable gulf between them. On the 20th February 1999, a crisp and sunny winter's day, the Bay was beautiful. The tense pair were waiting in suites high above the glittering waters. Rhodri was in the Snowdon Suite, Alun in the Lower Summit of Cader Idris Suite. Rhodri quipped that again he had 'the highest mountain to climb.'

Three and half months earlier, I was with them across the other side of the Bay. We were all doing live interviews for Sky television. Before the interview, the pair then struck a deal not to make personal attacks on each other. The deal lasted for the full election period.

Anyone expecting an inspirational occasion was disappointed. It was a bleak, down-beat shambles. Welsh Whip David Hanson Chaired the event. It was an experience he is unlikely to forget.

The mobile phone message said that Rhodri, Alun and the Wales Labour Party General Secretary, Anita Gale, had left the upstairs rooms. They were on their way to the lifts.

David had been instructed that he had exactly two minutes of introductory foreplay before the trio would majestically process into the

room. But the brand-new lifts had teething troubles and the trio had
walk down. David finished his two minutes of amiable babbling and su
fered the nightmare of all public speakers. He was on his feet with not
ing to say.

It's the time when a speaker thanks everyone, ' ... the women w
made the cakes, the vicar for the hire of the hall ...' David even me
tioned the date of the Assembly Election as 'May 7th'. 'No, the 6t
shouted the visibly irritated, impatient audience. David deserved
reward for his torment. He did not have to wait until he was in heav
to receive it.

In the first section, of Party members, Rhodri had won 64.4%
Alun's 35.6%. That was the only genuinely democratic Omov vo
Among Unions and affiliated organisation, Alun won, with 64%
Rhodri's 36%. In the third section, of MPs, MEPS and aspira
Assembly candidates, Alun had 58% to Rhodri's 42%.

The announcement cleaved the audience in two, Alun's support
quietly jubilant, Rhodri's deeply resentful. They avoided eye contact.

Neither candidate is an orator in the tradition of Lloyd George
Aneurin Bevan. Alun spoke first. He read from his script. It was as el
trifying and uplifting as a reading of the day's weather forecast, but l
relevant. He dreamed:

I will lead a united Labour Party in Wales because the will is the
The Wales Labour Party emerges healthier than ever from this electi
The Assembly must not be just about decisions and debate in a bui
ing in Cardiff. It must be about every part of Wales and about people
every part of Wales.

Probably unlike Alun, defeated Rhodri was hearing the figures for
first time. He was shocked by how close they were to claims Alu
camp a week earlier. He was convinced that he had been doub
crossed again. He managed to look relaxed:

I am getting used to doing these runner-up speeches, but I have
accept that, in spite of all the votes I got in the Trade Union section a
Party members, I have not won this contest. I don't feel like a lose
runner-up? Yes. A loser? Never.

A fire alarm went off and Rhodri joked that it was one of those
legged ducks. The laughter had a nervous edge. We were living
dreaded nightmare.

Rhodri had won a commanding lead in the democratic Omov v

members. He had the backing of twice as many Trade Unions as the ecretary of State. All those Unions which had conducted Omov balts had voted for Rhodri.

Even in the fiddled, bullied and stitched-up third section, Rhodri had on a substantial 42% of the total. Alun's victory margin would have sappeared if even one of the big Unions had chosen democracy. He ould also have lost if the list candidates had not been stitched-up.

The St David's Hotel became a Tower of Babel as the media interewed both camps. Ron Davies defended the stitch-up. He explained at all elements in the Labour Party deserve their share of the vote. The arty is really 'one large family' – rather like the mafia in this case.

Rhodri's friends seethed. We were six weeks away from the most difcult election Labour had faced in Wales for 20 years. The campaign was ready underway. An iron rule of politics is that you do not attack your arty at election time. We had two elections before us, Assembly and uropean.

No-one could give ammunition to our opponents by saying how ugry we were that Rhodri was cheated. Rhodri's friends wanted to imb up to the wing on the top of the St David's hotel and shout in nison to the heavens, 'STIIIIITCH-UP!'

We could not. We burbled pious platitudes. The truth was forbidden. hinking was treacherous. Our mouths were glued shut. That night, the abour Party in Wales was ashamed of itself. We were preparing our own tastrophe.

With their usual prescience, Wales on Sunday said:

This is a sad day for Welsh democracy. To have Wales's first 'Prime linister' elected in such blatantly unfair circumstances is not an occaons for celebration. Perhaps the happiest man is Dafydd Wigley.

Ceefax reported the result with a quote attributed to Tony Blair. It ay have been a mistake because it was very close to one previously edited to Alun. It provoked one Welsh MP to put the following on his ebsite that evening in the style of Rupert Bear.

Homage to Wales

By Rupert Blair

'The Welsh must put aside their dark, despairing Celtic side'
Tony Blair, February 20th 1999.

Hopeless, wretched little land,
Too sad, too Welsh to understand,
Forget your Mabinogion,
Ape the folk of Islington

To save you from mad kith and kin,
I have sent you Little Alun.
Your Celtic thoughts are dark and mixed
So his election I have fixed.

For your despair, I give you hope,
No need for you to try to cope
With home rule for your puny state,
From Downing Street I'll seal your fate.

Boyo-dom on Taff, Alun will run,
Lots of work, no joy, no fun
Rhodri wouldn't do at all,
Too bright and funny, and far too tall.

You gloomy Taffies, now rejoice
I've given you your own small voice,
An extra gift is this wise wish,
Be joyful, humble and - more English.

AFTERPLAY

*'History teaches us that men behave wisely once they have exhausted
all other alternatives'*

Abba Eban.

'CONGRATULATIONS to the member for Cardiff South on winning the election, and warm congratulations to the member for Cardiff West for winning three out of every four democratic votes cast' was the icy greeting from one Welsh MP on the Monday following the declaration.

It was delivered publicly, at a meeting of the Welsh Grand Committee held in equally icy, wind-swept Aberaeron. This was first chance for MPs to meet to chew over the events of the weekend. Rhodri Morgan had come to terms with the result, but something else was worrying him.

The statement he had made after the declaration mentioned 'the nightmare scenario' but he also called for work 'to unite the Party'. Employing his usual restraint, Tory Rod Richards had helpfully slammed what he called the 'biggest stitch-up of all time'. There's nothing like a Rod Richards attack to unite the Labour Party in Wales.

There was annoyance that the Party still preached, in a hand-out, the fiction that the electoral college was the same as that which elected Tony Blair. It was not. Then, Omov ruled all three sections. Had the same system been used, Rhodri would have been the runaway victor. Still no-one from Millbank has admitted the difference and its sinister intent.

What was ruining Rhodri's seaside awayday at wintry Aberaeron was the uncanny resemblance of the final result to the forecast made by Alun's team the week before. Had they been tipped off? When the result was announced, Rhodri said his 'eyes fell out of their sockets'. He had learned that the 35% to 65% figures were known in top Party and Union circles a week before. Their comments and body language told the same tale.

The press had noticed that Rhodri looked downcast when he arrived at the St David's Hotel before the announcement. Alun was described as having 'a neat haircut and his professorial glasses perched on his nose. He exuded the quiet confidence of the victor'.

As a seasoned campaigner, Rhodri knows the rules on how to behave in defeat. As Nye Bevan said, 'Never let your wounds show. They please your enemies and upset your friends'.

Rhodri was sensitive to the risk of being labelled a 'whinger' if he complained. But he owed it to his demoralised supporters to expose the ramshackle character of the voting procedure. No candidate or their representatives had the right to oversee the opening of the envelopes and counting of the votes. Rhodri's team still do not know when the votes were counted. Was there a running count as they arrived? Was a day stipulated to count them all? Why did the widely broadcast rumours of the result prove so uncannily accurate?

The balloting firm used in the Leadership election, Unity Security Balloting (USB), was set up by the Trade Unions following allegations of internal irregularities in several Union ballots. In this case, they answered to the Labour Party which had contracted them. Another doubt lingered to further poison trust. The date for dispatch of ballot forms to members had been brought forward without Rhodri's team being informed. Alun's caucus had taken advantage of insider information.

One additional double stitch in the ballot was noticed Geoff Mungham who a was member of Rhodri's campaign team:

'While ordinary party members returned their ballot papers to London, third sector voters of MPs, MEPs and Assembly candidates were required to return their ballot slip, along with their names and addresses to Transport House, home of the Labour Party Wales. Why was this? Surely it had nothing to do with a calculation that some nervous MPs and Assembly candidates, who had privately indicated their intention to vote for Morgan, might change their minds if they thought there was the faintest chance of having their vote identified?'

The parliamentary Labour Party changed their rules because of similar situations. Some MPs handed their ballot papers for shadow cabinets elections to the whips to vote on their behalf. This was a proof that they were willing to exchange their choice of candidate in order to gain favours from the whips. USB's procedures appeared to be less than professional and open to tampering. As a past observer of elections in Bulgaria, I know they would not pass muster by observers from other countries. The safeguards were not water tight. Rhodri did the minimum and made a written detailed complaint.

He was answered with a dismissive 32 word assurance from USB that the ballot was carried out 'secretly and fairly'. An unnamed Millbank apparatchik lashed back and denounced Rhodri as a 'whinger'. Millbank said the majority of Labour members in Wales 'don't want to waste time over an election that everyone accepts had one winner'. Everyone? 'Complete confidence' was expressed in the ballot.

The technique is familiar. If you have no defence to the argument, attack the opponent. Millbank's reply was a vacuous bluster with a sting for Rhodri. It was no answer to the serious charges made. There is no longer an election to distract us. A full answer and a reform of the processes are overdue.

There had been bitter recriminations against USB a year earlier concerning amazing coincidences involving the vote for the National Executive of the Labour Party. An apparent leak a few weeks before voting closed forecast that four candidates from the 'Grassroots Alliance' would win and only two from the Blairist 'Members First' slate. That was widely interpreted as a deliberate attempt to gee-up the non-activists who had not yet voted to vote the Blairist ticket. The forecast was spookily accurate.

Mark Seddon, editor of Tribune and an NEC member, had criticised USB at the time. The Labour Party bit back with a draconian ban. The National Executive Committee ordered that:

Any public attack on the balloting process will be seen as an attempt to influence the outcome of the ballot and will render the candidate concerned liable for exclusion from the ballot.

MP John Cryer said 'Trying to gag people in this way is deeply unfair and goes against the best democratic tradition of the Labour Party'.

Stories that Alun had won were not confined to the journalist, mentioned above, who said that he was told in a television studio on the eve of the declaration that Alun had won by 5%. I have had very convincing claims that information about the way in which members were voting was received on a daily basis by a top Alun campaigner. I cannot prove that. A detailed investigation might prove it is not true. But details are not forthcoming on this election or on the similar claims about the 1998 National Executive elections. No election should ever be conducted in this way again.

The Western Mail's Mike Settle had some interesting revelations in his epitaph to the campaign.

Never has there been such uncomradely behaviour among the comrades than over the past few weeks, with both briefing bitterly against the other.

Most of the supporters of either camp begin or end their conversation with the words, 'You can use it but don't use my name'. Such has been the extent of the poisoned arrows that some reporters have been rung up and told tales about each candidate's families. Needless to say, nothing of this nature has appeared in print but depths have been plumbed by some shady people.

Ron Davies was very chipper about the result and defended the conduct of the election. He was joined in that opinion by Ray Powell MP for Ogmore later in the Commons. Previously, they had not always agreed. He was in an informative mood with the press and revealed two previously unknown facts about himself. He is the great grandson of a mole-catcher and he was kept in the dark by Blair on government policy. The two facts are unconnected, but he revealed that he heard about new government policies on the radio while eating his cornflakes. He said it is the same thing with Alun Michael because that's the way the Whitehall mindset works.

Relaxed and confident, he may have pondered two outcomes highly satisfactory to him. Alun could still fail to win an Assembly seat. Then he could win the Leadership from Rhodri. Or, Labour might fail to gain 31 seats. The election of the Welsh Prime Minister would then have to rely on members of minority parties.

Ron's backing for Alun now was not as fulsome as his support during the election. When asked about the possibility of Alun being usurped, Ron said 'I do not have any comment to make'. Not the ringing endorsement he was happy to give himself. 'I still have a lot of ideas', he suggested, 'a very clear vision, a very clear set of proposals about how the Assembly should develop its own dynamism'.

Five months had already passed since the walk on Clapham Common. Ron's thoughts were on an Assembly without Alun. On Newsnight he confirmed that it was up to elected AMs to chose their own leader. Was there a gleam in his eye that said, 'it still may be me'?

Rhodri and I did not share his optimism. The day before the result was announced, we were lobbied by farmers on a hill overlooking large areas of mine and Ron's constituencies. Many journalists from the national press were present, ready to cover the vote next day.

When the farmers realised who the journalists were, they lost interest in giving Rhodri and me earache on the suckler cow premiums. They lined up with salacious stories of alleged incidents involving Ron. They used the vantage point to indicate the car parks and woods that featured in their tales.

The bad mouthing of Ron by Gwent farmers was not new. Ron had courageously challenged his farming neighbours on fox hunting. As a result of his stand, Ron was threatened with having a dead cow dumped in his garden. One incident took Ron and the farmers to court. A fox from another part of Gwent was imprisoned in a milk churn in Newport for three days. He was released on hunt day in full view of the hounds, chased across the countryside and torn to pieces.

The truth came to light because a spectator was sickened by this legalised sadism. The chase was long and greatly enjoyed. That was a vivid illustration of the bloody foul truth of foxhunting. A living creature, that suffers fear and pain as we do, was abused for fun.

Ron won his day in court. It was expensive for the hunters concerned and they have not forgiven him. It was bad news for Ron that they were now in hot pursuit of him.

Was it only a matter of time before a new scandal broke?

How to Lose a Campaign

'Anyone who isn't confused doesn't really understand the situation'
Ed Murrow.

THE LABOUR WELSH ARMY sleepwalked into battle. The first election, ever, for an all-Wales body. There was a Welsh Parliament of sorts in 1404, but Owen Glyndwr had similar views to Tony Blair on the value of democracy in Wales. There was some belief that the internal warfare was over and we could now all charge in the same direction at the common enemies. We were marching into an elephant trap of our own making.

The UK opinion polls were riding high for Labour, the voters of Wales had been super-loyal for a century. Surely a stitch-up or two could not alter ingrained voting patterns? We see ourselves as natural winners in Wales. How could we fail in the Assembly elections, especially with star campaign manager Peter Hain in charge and Don Touhig as his deputy? There had been so so many recent successes against the loathed Tories we had forgotten the failures.

Labour is still wedded to the doctine of Mandelsonian infallibility. A study of the Pontypridd by-election in 1989 could have helped. We were about to repeat all its errors in 1999 - Wales wide. The lesson of Peter Mandelson's other greatest failure had also been forgotten.

His tactics destroyed Labour's chance of winning a by-election at Littleborough and Saddleworth in 1995. It was good Labour territory which we eventually won in 1997. But Mandelson adopted an odd tactic. Sometimes the worst form of defence is attack - when it's against the wrong target.

At the time of the Tories' deepest unpopularity, Mandelson decided that the election should be fought on an anti-Liberal ticket. Most people vote against the Party they hate, rather than for the Party they love.

Why should they hate the popular local Councillor, Lib Dem candidate Chris Davies?

Labour dug deep for a bit of dirt on him. The worst they unearthed was a speech he made to the Lib Dems' Conference advocating a Royal Commission on Cannabis use. Mandelson used this weapon to beat up the Liberals. It was repeated on every day of the campaign.

Davies was demonised as a drug pushing libertine. In contrast, Peter canonised the Labour candidate, a former leader of the National Union of Students, as an immaculate hermit. The Tories were ignored. The voters decided that the Lib Dems had been caught in possession of an intelligent argument and elected Chris Davies. Labour was rejected on the grounds of implausible sanctity. Mandelson's tactics probably lost a winnable seat for Labour.

The Pontypridd by-election followed the loss of Glasgow Govan to the Scottish nationalists in 1989. The Labour candidate there had been destroyed by the merciless by election coverage. He was exposed a inadequate to the challenge from the greatly experienced Scottish nationalist, Jim Sillars.

Some genius decided that there was a nationalist bandwagon rolling from Scotland to Wales. It had to be stopped. In the words of the Tory candidate in Pontypridd, Nigel Evans, Labour was 'scared witless'.

Thatcher was still in power. The poll tax was in force and wildly hated. A campaign to say 'No to Thatcher' or 'No to the poll tax' would have been a winner. Instead, Labour had one theme: Hammer the Nats

Plaid Cymru were so delighted with Plaid-bashing leaflets, they distributed them themselves. Rightly, they said they proved that they were the alternative to Labour. With an unpopular local Labour Council, th voters happily switched to Plaid.

The campaign gave them the choice: 'Vote Plaid against an unpopular Labour Council', not: 'Vote Labour against an unpopular Tory government'. The nationalist vote jumped from 5% to 25%. Had Labour campaigned harder, or if the election had continued for another fortnight, Plaid could have won.

Undeterred, this tactic was the model for the Welsh Labour Party Assembly campaign. The plan was to polarise the election between Labour and the nationalists. Incredible as it may seem, the belief was that the people could be persuaded to come out on May 6th and vote against Plaid by voting Labour. The megalomania of election manager had slipped into dementia.

Two depressing polls for Labour were eloquent Cassandras. A survey of Party Leaders' popularity had Alun on 29%, and Dafydd Wigley on 28%. The other Parties' Leaders were on the ludicrous level of 9% for Tory Rod Richards and 5% for Lib Dem Mike German.

The forecasts of Rhodri's glummest supporters were vindicated. One poll in the run-up to the Leadership ballot gave him a nine-to-one lead over Alun. Ieuan Wyn Jones, the nationalist MP for Ynys Mon and the Party's Assembly campaign co-ordinator, trumpeted Wigley as the only politician of the necessary stature to act as Wales's 'national leader'.

The seven weeks of campaigning were kicked off by Labour with a blistering attack. On Rod Richards? No. On Dafydd Wigley. Rubbishing Rod would have gone with the grain of public opinion. Convincing the nation that avuncular Dafydd was 'Wrigley Wigley' was a suicidal tactic. The opinion poll confirmed that thousands of people in Wales who had never voted nationalist preferred Dafydd to Alun. Dafydd was a familiar figure and respected as a campaigner for the disabled. What prospect was there of destroying that image in a few weeks?

Worse was to come. A Millbank importee produced an A-to-Z guide to 'nationalist Madness'. It's dangerous to trap yourself into finding a weakness in opponents for every letter of the alphabet. It ranged from A for Airlines' – 'the separatists say that Wales needs its own national airline which, Labour says, would cost £200m to establish' – to 'Z for Zealots' – 'The nationalists are zealots whose views are not shared by the vast majority of people in Wales'.

Two examples of Plaid's 'madness' quoted were their wish to replace student loans with grants, and their policy to increase the basic pension in line with the level of earnings, not prices. That's the kind of insanity most Welsh voters find irresistible. Why were Labour advertising Plaid's most popular policies? Had someone in Labour Party Wales taken a swing from Plaid?

Alun hit the nail on the head. 'The nationalist tactic', he said, 'was to look like Labour only a little more cuddly' – especially to students and pensioners. Plaid's Karl Davies said, 'This is good news: it really puts a smile on my face'.

To deal with the problem of Alun's invisibility, a strategy was devised to use the first half of the election to establish Alun Michael as a Leader. The second half would concentrate on destroying Plaid Cymru. This was later changed. Halfway through, the genius who was running the show decided that, as Labour was doing so well, the whole campaign period should concentrate on fitting out Alun with a personality.

Some people still had a grip on reality. One Gwent constituency Party campaign team made two firm decisions at their first meeting. The 'A–Z of nationalist Madness' was never to be distributed. After pondering the pulling power of the Party leaders, they decided that neither Alun's nor Tony Blair's face should appear on their election literature. That constituency enjoyed a good Labour result.

Kirsty Milne, writing in the Scotsman, captured the mood of Labour voters. She spent a day with Chris Llewellyn, candidate for the crucial Carmarthen East and Dinefwr seat. He had to lose to get Alun in with a list place. During the day, she observed an animated conversation entirely in Welsh. 'The only words intelligible to me', Kirsty wrote, 'were 'Tony Blair' (said indignantly), 'Alun Michael' (said disgustedly) and 'Rhodri Morgan' (said with an air of ownership). Chris Llewellyn listened patiently. His parting shot was 'John Prescott!' (said with an air of desperation)'.

Chris Llewellyn was a Rhodri supporter. He said that when Rhodri came to town,' ... people's faces lit up, they wanted to go out and talk to him'. With Alun, it was not quite the same. Someone from Hitchcock Horror Casting had hired (from England!) a sinister all-black bus as campaign wagon. Even the windows were black. Voters emptied the streets when it approached. The 'Daily Post' reported that 'the battlebus became caught up in a funeral cortege'. Onlookers said it was a fitting vehicle for the occasion.

There was a further embarrassment. A press release put out by Alun in the Mid and West Wales constituency mentioned local Labour candidates Ann Garrard and Chris Gwyther but omitted Chris Llewellyn's name. At that stage, no-one guessed that Ann Garrard was vulnerable in her Llanelli Labour stronghold. 'Spin Doctor' observed 'I am sure the omission is nothing whatever to do with the fact that if Chris wins, Alun is very unlikely to get a seat'. Of course not. Another Labour leaflet sent a chill down the spines of the elderly in West Wales promising that Labour had an 'exiting' strategy for pensioners.

The purse strings were now open wide for a lavish campaign. Money that was un-available for an Omov ballot which would have given Rhodri victory, magically sprung from the empty purse. The election

ending by Labour was reported to be £1 million plus. But vote buy-
ng is no longer is a weapon against the valley to valley 'disgust' that
Guardian write Matthew Engel found:

There is profound bitterness. Disgust is truly the word at the grubby
x which secured the leadership of Welsh Labour for Alun Michael. This
as done more damage to Mr Blair's reputation in Wales than he can
magine.

There was another sickening, demoralising blow to Party activists. In
is usual good natured way, Rhodri had forgotten his wounds and cam-
aigned alongside Alun in a show of unity. There was an armistice in the
arty Civil War until the elections were over. But peace had been
eclared on one side only. Alun's lot were at it again. Stitching up had
ecome addictive. They had not had a 'fix' for three weeks. As with all
ddicts, their bodies cried out, just one more, ... a final fix.

It was Plan B in the event of Alun failing to gain a list seat. The cau-
us fretted that the freshly elected AMs might not chose a New Labour
ternative. After all, the candidates were predominately Rhodri sup-
orters. Under the prevailing system it was their choice alone.

So the rules were torn up. A new system was announced. The future
ader was to be chosen by a college of elected AMs plus 30 members
f the obedient Welsh Executive. The calculation was that the predom-
ance of Dragons amongst new AMs would be out-voted by the
xecutive Poodles to select an Alun act-alike, think-alike, fawn-alike.

Party members judged it to be the final dirty trick to frustrate any
ossibility of Leadership bids by Rhodri or Ron Davies. The wounds of
justice were re-opened. Even in victory, New Labour resisted the
mptation to be generous or magnanimous.

It was the last but most contemptuous stitch-up.

FROM THE BUNKER

'One more such victory and we are lost.'

Pyrrhus

WHEN ADOLF HITLER and his last surviving cronies were holed up in the bunker in Berlin in the final days of the war, they became deluded. They still sent out orders. Armies were ordered into battle. Targets were picked to bomb. Ships were instructed to leave harbour.

Directly above the bunker, the Russian soldiers were destroying Berlin. The delusion was maintained until reality intruded and they blew their brains out.

Election strategists from all Parties suffer similar delusions. They vastly exaggerate their own power to determine the result. Money spent here, canvassers dispatched there, a well phrased press statement, all, they believe, will transform voting intentions. Instructions from the Party's bunker will direct armies of Party workers to shore up the defences, or mount an attack. That's the faith that justifies the expensive existence of party election managers.

It's mostly poppycock. Because of today's mass disillusionment with party politics, the strategists are directing non-existent armies. The troops have deserted. They are not knocking doors. They are tucked up inside watching Frazier or The Simpsons.

Campaign managers for Labour and Plaid were tying their brains in knots deciding how to handle the Mid and West Wales constituencies, specially Carmarthen East and Dinefwr. Simon Hoggart of the Guardian tried to explain:

Plaid Cymru want to lose the seat to Labour. But official Labour wants to lose it too. Supporters of Rhodri Morgan, however, will be wholeheartedly backing Labour in order to squeeze Mr Michael out.

It's a confused situation, with the two main parties both ostensibly

wanting to win and privately wanting to lose, except for rebel element
in Labour, who are so rebellious that they want to win. It would be outrageous to suggest that Plaid Cymru and Labour are trying to help eacl
to win the seat, but I gather there have been many informal contacts
So all these incredibly complicated and manipulative arrangements ma
have the precise opposite effect to the one intended, and it would tak
a heart of stone not to be delighted.

A further complication was a tiny Labour group (possibly two peo
ple) who urged Labour supporters to vote once for Labour and then te
use their second vote to keep Alun out. Their connections with th
Party were disputed. If it was a stunt, it was a good one that gained
great deal of publicity.

Now, on the eve of the poll, it was the pollsters' turn to pontificate
HTV / NOP forecast an overall Labour majority of eight in the 60
member Assembly. Labour was predicted to win 34 seats, against 13 fc
Plaid Cymru, seven for the Conservatives and six for the Liber.
Democrats. Only one constituency would change hands compared wit
the 1997 election: Carmarthen East and Dinefwr would switch fror
Labour to Plaid Cymru's Rhodri Glyn Thomas.

More voters wanted Plaid Cymru's Dafydd Wigley to be Fir
Minister (42%) than believed Mr Michael to be the best man for the jo
(39%), a possible result of Labour talking Wigley down. A truism i
Welsh Labour circles is, 'Attack the Tories, their vote goes down: attac
Plaid, their vote goes up.'

The voters showed a healthy degree of cynicism. A large proportic
of them were convinced that all the Parties were lying. Half did n
believe the nationalists' disclaimer on independence not being their po
icy. Only 31% said they believed the Conservatives' claim that it w
work to make the Assembly a success. 31 % said they did not believ
that Welsh Labour would make its own decisions and not be run fro
London.

In the Rhondda, the Guardian's insightful Matthew Engel proved tl
folly of election forecasts, stating that 'If Wayne David was to lose,
would be a political earthquake that would bust the seismograph'. B
perceptively, he pinpointed the secret asset of the Plaid candidate.

Geraint Davies is a pharmacist in Treherbert. That means he n
merely knows a large proportion of the electorate, but knows the
innermost secrets as well. One fancies him having a unique system

voter classification in his head: 'Jones the gout'; 'Williams the haemor-rhoids'; 'Evans-not-worth-canvassing-because-he-might-not-last-till-polling-day'.

Peter Hain was not impressed. He was elated and handed out hostages to fortune as though he was dishing out smarties at a children's party. No hyperbole was left unsaid. 'The poll is a crushing blow to the other parties', he fulminated. 'If the results turn out as we expect it will be seen as a remarkable achievement'.

The next day, Peter was still in triumphalist mood. The day's results were going to be:

a major triumph for the Labour Party ... in the round, I defend every-thing we've done. No campaign or any document is ever perfect, but I think our assault (on Plaid) on independence and their attempts to clear their website have been very effective ... Plaid will have to examine its political ethos after this election. It's going to mean the death of Old Nationalism.

He was about to learn that 24 hours is an eternity in politics.

'I'VE LOST THE RHONDDA'

'The earth shall rise on new foundations'
The Internationale

ELECTION battle-hardened Wayne David looked strained.

Although the Assembly votes were not being counted until Friday morning, it was possible to judge the results with fair accuracy by observing the figures for the local Council elections held the same day. They were counted on the evening of Thursday May 6th.

Controversially, a decision had been made to leave the Assembly count to Friday. The Referendum count the previous year had dragged on until beyond 4.00 am, leaving bodies frazzled and emotions ravaged. This time, refreshed and lively politicians had the whole day to savour the full joys of the voters' approval.

But not Wayne David. He had abandoned his senior position in the Euro Labour Group and his Euro meal ticket for life, walking away from one of the biggest majorities in the Northern Hemisphere to try his luck in the Rhondda, which, at the previous General Election, had the second biggest Labour majority in the UK. A rumour rippled across Wales. Wayne David was reputed to have uttered, to a consenting friend in private, the chilling words 'I've just lost the Rhondda'.

Wayne had been dogged by complaints about the local Council. The Guardian reported what was meant to be a helpful comment by a supporter of the Rhondda Council:

It's a very widespread perception, but it's unfair. I could name you half a dozen Councils in Wales that are far more corrupt. This one's just incompetent.

Cognoscenti explained Wayne's fears away as the well known 'candidate's neurosis'. Often, depression and pessimism overwhelm candidates on election day. Wayne would not be the first to foresee defeat in the portents of certain victory. Few believed him.

147

Writing later, Matthew Engel described Wayne's nightmare:

> *In Treorchy and Treherbert and Trealaw the unthinkable was happen-*
> *ing. He knew he was done for. Wayne David went and told his wife,*
> *working for the Party at the big Cardiff count. She hugged him. Then,*
> *at 5am, he went home, made half a dozen cups of tea and worked out*
> *what he was going to say. There was no sleep. But when he got to the*
> *following day it was harder: he had to face his mam, who had rearranged*
> *a hip operation in the hope that she was going to meet the Queen.*

Labour was depressed about local Council results, but still faced that Friday morning of May 7th with optimism. Reacting for Labour on the TV panels that announced the results were three stalwarts of the stitch-up, two of then in the Alun-loop: Peter Hain, Don Touhig and Glenys Kinnock.

Perhaps the most eloquent statement of the whole day was the intake of breath by Glenys at the news that Labour had indeed lost the Rhondda. Don Touhig was on mission impossible in dredging up a comforting interpretation of the loss of his own constituency seat of Islwyn by his researcher, Shane Williams. The resilient Peter Hain occasionally sounded plausible while eating crow, plus a pile of his own words.

These programmes are our closest modern equivalent to the Mediaeval Inquisition. The torture is subtler but more public. The merciless eye of the camera relays to millions all tear filled eyes, each quivering lip and every downcast face.

That day is fixed in the memories of most viewers by the expressive faces of the panels and the candidates. Ron Davies looked troubled at the tiny turn-out in Caerphilly and his slashed majority. That was the first result declared. By the time the news came from other pulverised Welsh valley constituencies, Ron's result looked triumphant. Wayne, pale and shocked, was stoical and emotionless, standing to attention with his hands clasped behind his back. Rhodri beamed angelically. His consolation was a triumphantly vast bouquet of votes from Cardiff West He had the biggest Labour majority and he was the only Labour candidate to improve on the record-breaking '97 result. Lib Dems Kirsty Williams glowed with optimism in Brecon, the pleasant face of new young Wales.

Visibly upset, Labour's Ann Garrard at Llanelli was fighting emotions of resentment, betrayal and frustration. Tory Leader Rod Richards's face was distorted with disappointment and embarrassment at losing the Conservatives 'safest' seat in Wales for the second time.. The alleged wild man of Scotland, Dennis Canavan, was quietly conciliatory. He had challenged expulsion by New Labour and won Scotland's biggest majority as an Independent MSP.

The final grim Welsh result for the 60 seats was: Labour 28 seats; Plaid 17; Conservatives 9; and Lib Dems 6. Labour were three seats short of an overall majority. The General Election result two years earlier for 40 seats was Labour 34, Plaid 4, Conservatives 0 and Lib Dems 2. There were astonishing wins for the nationalists in Llanelli, Islwyn and the Rhondda. They added to their joy by gaining control of both Rhondda Cynon Taff and Caerphilly Councils from Labour.

Bookmakers had been offering 20-1 against a Plaid win in Rhondda. The swing there was more than 30 %. This was Doomsday, a catastrophe for Labour. Would New Labour now accept that they had done something wrong?

The first signs were not good. The three television pundits floundered at first. This was not in the script. Media junkies train themselves beforehand to cope plausibly with every eventuality. They mouth their delicately phrased, measured reactions. They had not practised for End of the World.

A sane response to these horror results would have been to run sobbing from the set. No, no. Our three apologists for Labour's ruin toughed it out. Peter Hain was the first to recover. 'I've warned for over a year', said Peter, 'that the Labour Party in Wales shouldn't be complacent about this election'.

The little known Welsh broadcaster Betsan Powys deployed some penetrative irony when, with a fetching smile, she asked Peter Hain, 'So, you're losing out of the goodness of your own hearts, then, are you?'

In the following two days, Peter refined his self-justifying alibi. The only consolation was the 'election' of Alun through the assisted places PR scheme. It was a victory bought at high cost. Two Labour seats had been sacrificed to Plaid. In the opening lines of his speech to the Labour Party Conference at Bournemouth in September, Alun described himself as the 'First Ever Elected Leader of Wales'. Elected? Perhaps. Democratically elected? Perhaps not.

Not a word of remorse or confession of failure came from Labour's Cardiff Bunker. They decided to fake it again. Millbank groupies and Party hacks painstakingly rehearsed their 'spontaneous' ecstatic welcome for Alun. It is the New Labour mindset of denial. When confronted with disaster, convince everyone else it's a triumph.

Alun, the victorious, heroic conqueror was feted. He gave a press Conference at the Party's Cathedral Road Headquarters, flanked by a semicircle of big-name Labour grandees. He had the right country in his speech, but it was not the Gettysburg address. 'It's an historic day for Wales', he announced, ' ... a National Assembly for Wales, making decisions for Wales, for the future of Wales, for the people of Wales, taken here in Wales'.

Oh, for a one-legged duck.

Shape Shifter

'For Brutus is an honourable man,
So are they all, honourable men'

Shakespeare.

PETER HAIN became New Labour personified.

Energetically, he fought to get his fiction in first. Explaining the reason for defeat, he suggested that 'the Labour Party has been gratuitously offensive to its traditional supporters'.

Was this Peter Hain related to the Peter Hain who had disparaged Rhodri's supporters as 'crypto-nationalists' and 'Trotskyists'? He spoke critically of 'control freakery'. What next? Would Jack the Ripper volunteer for Neighbourhood Watch?

He was brimming over with excuses. 'Our poor showing in some of these Labour heartland areas', spun Peter, 'was local Council issues more than anything else'. Possibly the Welsh Office failure to get a grip on Councils' DLOs?

Peter even complained that the brief six weeks from February 20th did not give him enough time to convince the voters. Peter was gambling that Wales had already forgotten that he was the author of Alun's leadership campaign timetable, elongated to help Alun in the hope of a Rhodri gaffe.

Next, Peter published an article in the Western Mail explaining how he had long ago diagnosed the problems of the Labour Party in Wales. It was a whole three days since he had forecast that the Assembly elections would be ' ... a major triumph for the Labour Party'. He was relying on the belief that the public has the attention span of an earthworm.

Not a word was uttered by the campaign manager that the campaign was not managed perfectly. Certainly, no hint from the manipulator of the stitch-ups that they may have disillusioned tens of thousands of

Labour voters.

Peter has tiptoed deftly from left to right in politics, then back again. He took the Welsh Office job that should have gone to Rhodri Morgan. This is a politician of extraordinary versatility. After master minding the loss of Llanelli, Islwyn and the Rhondda, he was immedi ately back lecturing the nation that bad was good, loss was gain, fix wa fair.

In Star Trek, there is a shape-shifter named Odo. He is infinitely mal leable. He liquefies at the end of each day into a gelatinous mass an sleeps in a bucket. The following morning he emerges in any shape h desires. Odo was the only one of his kind in the Alpha quadrant. Ha Peter modelled his political persona on Odo? Today, shining Nev Labour: tomorrow, Revolutionary Progressive.

Early in the year, Peter published a booklet entitled 'The Third Way Tribune unkindly suggested that the 'h' was silent. The booklet wa shape-shifting in its purest form. His hymn of praise extended from th dictatorial centralism of New Labour to the co-operative success c Tyrone O'Sullivan's pit. That's the same Tyrone who was judged as unf to be considered as an Assembly candidate by New Labour dictatori centralism.

Leighton Andrews, the lobbyist, heaped praise on Peter's booklet. Th is the same Leighton Andrews who was given a place on a quango b William Hague in 1996. Leighton then shifted shape and was one c 'Alun's supporters' on a BBC Wales TV debate during the Leadershi election.

Andrews drooled that 'Hain has little time for the Old Labour fixer of Wales'. Not then, anyway. Peter was busy honing the skills of Nev Labour fixing. Leighton wrote that 'Peter believes in mutual support Indeed. A week later, Peter wrote a foreword to Leighton's latest bool effusively supporting Leighton's prose. We were beginning to get th message of mutuality.

New Labour and Old Lobbyists hand in hand, guiding us all towar the New Jerusalem.

NEMESIS

'Gwae i wlad Gymru druan, O dir Lloegr deuai'r llygraid'— *'Pitiful land, poor Wales. Corruption came from England'*.
Ieuan Brydydd Hir XVIII Century

THE PARTY in Wales was now a basket case.

We had spent nine months in hell and we were assailed by guilt, self-doubt and insecurity. The safest seats had been lost. Some best friends were now enemies. Lost and disorientated, we were now marooned in the middle of another election campaign.

The Cardiff and Millbank bunkers descended deeper underground, even further from reality. The queen bees still sent out the orders to a phantom army of worker bees. MPs were horrified to have a cubic metre of election literature dumped on their driveways. Millbank dispatched 63 million leaflets to local parties.

I begged for mercy and explained that I was converting my garage to a granny flat. There was no place to store Euro leaflets. I told them that, in clearing out the garage, I had filled a skip with undelivered election literature from three previous Euro-campaigns. Why not cut out the middleman this time and deliver the cubic metre straight to the tip?

In Wales, bruised, insulted Party workers refused to campaign for candidates that they had not chosen. Nor did they want to work under a leader who had been imposed on them. The public hostility on the streets to Euro-canvassers that was the worst I have known since 1983.

Only the payroll vote could be press-ganged into life. The canvassing and street-stall groups I took part in were staffed by Party officials, Party office-holders, MPs and their families.

It would be a surprise if as many as 1% of the printed leaflets were distributed in Wales. Leaflets are now useless. Nearly all are thrown away as junk mail by recipients. A survey I did, some years ago, revealed that only one person in ten reads campaign leaflets. That's not one person in ten of those who receive them, it's one in ten of those who distribute them.

This truth was embarrassingly underlined in my constituency in this Euro election. Leaflets were delivered, not by Newport West members but in Newport West, promising that 'Labour would work in Europe for Scotland.' QED, the deliverers had not read the leaflets.

Even candidates are sometimes shielded from the truth. Glenys Kinnock was fired up with enthusiasm in her first election as a Euro candidate in 1994. As an old lag of all the Euro votes since 1979, I tried to cool her expectations of a lively campaign with a dose of realism. Her ultimate election with a huge majority was assured. John Major was PM, Glenys was a perfect candidate and the voters ached to give the Kinnock family a vote of consolation after the hammering of Neil in 1992.

The Party workers were unmoved, locked into their traditional Euro rigor mortis of inactivity. Glenys visited Newport West on polling day. In an act of shame and kindness, a Party worker toured Glenys's planned route the night before. A dozen Party members were begged, bullied or blackmailed into putting up window bills.

Glenys was mildly impressed by the show. No-one explained that on her brief trip around the patch, she had seen almost every window bill that was on display throughout the Newport West constituency.

By 1999, Neil was well consoled and there was no Tory PM to insult. Just as the Party in Wales was staggering to its feet after the Assembly result beating, we were floored again by an inevitable Euro kicking. Some optimistic souls had consoled themselves that voters deserted Labour because they were anti-devolution, or because they preferred Plaid for a Wales-only election. The Euro vote proved that the flirtation with Plaid was no one-night stand. Labour's seat tally dropped from MEPs to 2, partly because of PR. Plaid Cymru took 2 seats with a terrifying 29.6% of the Welsh vote, even higher that the share they had won in the Assembly election.

In the universal gloom of the Party in the UK following the Euro elections, few noticed the second sharp caning that Welsh voters had given Labour. The House of Commons Library analysis proves that was not only an anti-Euro backlash in Wales, it was anti-Labour Party.

Turnout cannot be blamed. Apart from Northern Ireland, Wales had

e highest turnout of the European 'electoral regions' with 28%. The
largest constituency turn-outs were in Wales. Wales also experienced
e highest swing against Labour: 23% compared to 16% in England and
% in Scotland. Wales also had four of the five largest constituency
ings against Labour in the UK: Neath with 32%, Swansea East 33%,
ondda 33% and Islwyn 35%.

Labour's Welsh nightmare was more ghastly than that in Scotland or
gland. The only plausible explanation was the still smarting insult of
e stitch-up of Rhodri. Would the lessons be learnt?

There were hopeful signs. We had technically 'won' Cardiff Central in
e Euro vote after losing it in the Assembly vote. The seat has never
en safe for any party. Tory Minister Ian Grist was replaced as MP by
bour's Jon Owen Jones in 1992. The Lib-Dems, who have long had a
ong local authority presence in Cardiff Central, gained the Assembly
it in 1999, Jenny Randerson defeating Labour's Mark Drakeford. In
e view of one local member, Labour lost it because of the turmoil of
e stitch-up. He wrote:

There was no effective Key Seat strategy. Jenny Randerson picked up
tensive media coverage as a 'Spokesperson' for the Lib Dems. Labour
ndidate Mark Drakeford, though by far the most able candidate, was
ver given an opportunity for media exposure. I was struck by how
any times in media debates we put up Alun Michael and Peter Hain
d how few chances were given to our key Assembly candidates.
onically, the frequent appearances of Alun and Peter were, in my view,
ten counter-productive, since they served to remind people about the
adership issue. The 'Rhodri' factor undoubtedly cost us votes.

The lesson of the success in 1997 of Labour's key seats strategy had
en eclipsed by the need to establish the authority of Alun as a Leader.
might have worked had Labour won well. The Welsh Group of
bour MPs reached similar conclusions to the party member in Cardiff
entral. The Group had been a battleground for more than a year. Now
were less combative, united by shared calamity. The shock of defeat
is profound, especially to those whose constituencies had fallen to
aid Cymru.

No spinning or shape-shifting could obscure the awful truth. A 15-
% swing to Plaid in all seats and Labour's lowest share of the vote
ice 1983. It was our lowest Euro share ever and, although higher than
e national average, turnout was the smallest in Wales since the

introduction of adult suffrage.

The group of Welsh Labour MPs decided to conduct a rational analysis of our unprecedented drop in votes. I urged the group to examine the swings against Labour in all seats. By far the best results for Labour in the Assembly elections, where Labour's vote held up most strongly, were those of Rhodri and of his main advocate in North Wales, John Marek. The largest decreases in Labour's support were in Torfaen, Swansea East, Merthyr Tydfil & Rhymney, Islwyn, Pontypridd and Llanelli. Four of those six swings were suffered by prominent declared supporters of Alun. There was also remarkable consistency between the Assembly and Euro results. In the Euro poll, Plaid 'won' in all the seats they had gained in the Assembly election.

The constituencies identified most closely with Rhodri Morgan and Old Labour had achieved the best results. Those nearest to New Labour had suffered the worst. We had won the Assembly Elections as Old Labour. Would we now rule as Old Labour? On this point, a state of hysterical myopia exists.

The causes suggested by MPs for the calamity were the rigging of the Leadership election, mid-term disappointment with the government, unpopular Councils, a poor campaign by the Party, the demoralisation and disaffection of Party workers caused by the enforced twinning and lack of democratic accountability in the Euro election. The key poll that said that Rhodri as leader would deliver a 9% improvement in Labour share of the vote was recalled. Added to that was the widespread disillusionment with the final result of the Alun-Rhodri election.

In electoral terms Rhodri was a positive factor: Alun, a negative one. If Rhodri had been Leader, it is a statistical certainty that Labour would have won Llanelli, Islwyn, and Conwy. That would have given Labour an overall majority in the Assembly. Control of the Assembly was the main political price of the stitch-up. Using the election to boost Alun as Leader was accentuating the negative and driving voters into the hands of Plaid. How could the fabled electoral skills of New Labour crash so abjectly?

Denouncing Plaid as mad for supporting pensioners and students was crass. Our offer of free bus fares for the elderly had its merits but it came across as an unconvincing bribe. No use where there is a poor, or no bus service. No help to the elderly who are too frail or disabled to use buses and irritating to those pensioner families struggling to maintain car on dwindling assets. Free bus fares are a poor substitute for Plaid's policy of raising the basic pension in line with the level of earnings.

Mid-term blues was not a convincing excuse. The popularity of Tony Blair and the government was high elsewhere in the UK. The effect of local Council scandals could not explain away the huge swings. In some areas with major scandals, Labour did very well - in the Vale of Glamorgan and in Blaenau Gwent, for example. A 14% increase in Council Tax was blamed for the Islwyn disaster. But in neighbouring Newport West and East, even though the increase had been 15%, both Assembly seats were won convincingly. Two new local anti-Council parties in Newport did only minor damage.

I was amazed to find myself moving the final report of Welsh MPs on the analysis of the failure. It acknowledged that 'any future leadership election must be conducted on the basis of Omov' and that the Welsh executive must be re-structured. The report identified the prime reason for electoral failure as the ''perception' of a fix, a stitch-up' arranged by London, Millbank and Tony Blair. There was an acknowledgement that our core vote resented 'apparent' interference in what should have been Welsh choice for Welsh elections.

The contingency comfort words 'apparent' and 'perception' were accepted because the stitchers were bowed down with remorse. The party was battered, bruised, bewildered, searching for solace. Is there such a thing as a Spin Psychiatrist?

I Chose You

THE OPENING of the Welsh Assembly was unforgettable. The Llandaff Cathedral Service and the Cardiff Bay Concert were proof that someone had been thinking anew to create two unique, thrilling and joyous events.

Our emotions melted with pride in Wales. At Llandaff, Wales put on its many cultured face. The country's second anthem, 'Dros Gymru'n Gwlad' (For Wales, our Country), was deeply moving. And who had the courage at the Bay to blend rock songs with mediaeval poetry? It was a night of excitement, laughter and beauty - plus a wonderful flaming dragon.

But even in the solemnity of the service, a slight sour aroma was detectable among the cathedral smells of candle grease, book mould and incense. The whiff of the stitch-up lingered. Alun's legitimacy as First Secretary was raised. Amazingly, it came from the lips of Alun himself. Was it sabotage or just a cock-up? Alun's bible reading contained a candid confession. The congregation shuddered at the words. Without a stumble or a blush, he read from the epistle of John, Chapter 15: 'You did not choose me. I chose you'.

Amen, to that.

Foul-Ups, or Stitch-Ups?

'Election cheating is no gamble: history is written by winners'
11th Precept of Pompom-ism.

The Welsh Labour Party is not fully representative of the people. We do not have a fair proportion of villains and crooks. But some of the many honest people in the Party have been caught out behaving like charlatans. The intention of this book is to cast a searchlight over some murky places in the hope that they will never be visited by our Party again.

Some stitch-ups had principled aims, but were achieved by questionable means. Others were unprincipled in concept and execution. Briefly they are:

TWINNING

Principled aim: To ensure equal numbers of female and male candidates in all constituencies, in order to correct the atrocious under representation of Welsh women.

Unprincipled means: Bulldozed through Welsh Conference by presenting a Hobson's choice of similar alternatives that denied opponents the chance to promote their objections.

Remedy: Should not be necessary in future elections.

EURO SELECTION

Unprincipled aims and means: Candidates who were not selected by Wales were forced on Wales. The all-important order of candidates also decided outside of significant Welsh influence by, predominantly, a loyalty test to New Labour. Choice of Lyndon Harrison over two local MEPs outraged the Party. Retreat was forced by united view of members.

Remedy: New selection system in which members have choice of nom
ination, selection and candidates' list order.

ELECTORAL COLLEGE

Unprincipled aim: Planned to ensure victory for Alun Michael by hoo
or (mostly) by crook.

Unprincipled means: Omov was used or ditched to suit Alun's advantag
Used in constituency section because GMC vote of activists would ha
favoured Rhodri even more than Omov did. Allowing Omov to b
dropped by Unions gave Union bosses power to determine results. A
Union Omov ballots chose Rhodri.

Remedy: Omov in all sections as pre-requisite to participation in ball

PANEL OF ASSEMBLY CANDIDATES SELECTION

Principled aim: To end past fixes by Trade Union bosses and others
achieve a balanced choice of candidates that would be representative
gender, ethnic group, business and disabled interests.

Maladroit means: Approved panel omitted many with first class qualific
tions and downgraded value of long service to the Party. Left limit
choice to many constituencies, which was reduced still further by twi
ning.

Remedy: Admission for consideration by constituencies of all aspira
candidates, except the obviously sad, mad or bad.

ADDITIONAL CANDIDATES

Mixed aims: Good: to add those who were wrongly excluded. Bad:
add candidates with influence in high places.

Unprincipled means: Appeals panel accepted previously rejected can
dates without providing reasons, well founded suspicions of patrona
persist – integrity of original choice wrecked.

LIST SEATS

Unprincipled aim: To avoid defeat for Alun in two out of the th sections of the electoral college.

Unprincipled means: Third section was corrupted by imposing Michael supporters on lists, against the wishes of constituencies. Bitterly resented open use of bullying by Party apparatchiks and Executive members.

Remedy: Replace with a fair PR system where list order is decided by preferences to best losers in first past the post constituency election. Elimination of candidates who fail to gain constituency nominations, thus ending unfair Party patronage.

ELECTION OF LEADER

Unprincipled aim: To deny elected AMs the choice of Leader and maintain power to select in the hands of Downing Street. Precautionary move to prepare for failure of Alun Michael to win seat and to ensure that Rhodri or Ron Davies were not chosen by AMs.

Unprincipled means: Rule book was torn up. New method of electing leader was to be by newly invented college of AMs plus 30 members of (Blairist-controlled) Welsh Executive.

Remedy: Ensure that electoral systems cannot be manipulated to serve interests of individual candidates.

UNION BALLOTS

Unprincipled aim: To allow Union barons to override their members' democratic rights.

Unprincipled means: Outrageous secrecy in which many large Unions reached their decisions has been denounced by many of their own members. A large cloud still hangs over conduct of crucial GMB vote.

Remedy: Disregard all ballots that are not Omov or are not open to independent scrutiny.

CONDUCT OF LEADERSHIP BALLOT

Grounds for serious concern: Would not have been approved as fair by UN observers of an election in a Third World country. Procedures were wide open for manipulation. Information denied to (some?) candidates, scrutiny by candidates or agents of the opening or counting of ballot papers not allowed. Powerful rumours indicated a possible leak of intelligence on voting results to one side. It is alleged that Alun's team were receiving daily reports of the changing vote count in the final days. A call for an explanation and investigation have been contemptuously swept aside. Even worse, a draconian, Stalinist new rule was imposed threatening disqualification for candidates who criticise the conduct of the poll.

Remedy: Major reform of procedures to allow surveillance of all stages of the ballot by independent observers plus representative of all candidates.

TRUE MEETS NEW

'We should not rely on parliamentary activity but also on extra parliamentary forces including the trade unions and the womens movement.'

Peter Hain 1989

TONY BLAIR argued at the Welsh Labour Conference in 1999 that the Party is a happy united band of sisters and brothers. Others' claims that there are differences between the old and the young, the left and the right, the traditional and the modern are 'complete rubbish'.

General Blair is fighting previous wars. Understandably so. Internal divisions have previously wrecked Labour governments. But he undervalues the demoralisation of Classic Labour who refuse to be displaced or anaesthetised by Millbank's Midwitch Socialists.

One of the most beneficial reforms in the party has been the progress made by women in recent years. The increase in the numbers of women MPs has been a triumph. But there has also been a lively clash of cultures between some of Labour's liberated women and Millbank's apparatchiks.

Prior to the 1997 General Election, the Party treasured its key seat candidates and lavished resources on them. They were to be our champions on the battlefields where Labour's victory was to be won. One of them, from a Midlands seat, described her experience for me in the following terms:

ENCOUNTER ONE:

During a session designed to advise us on how to handle the media, I was told to 'lose two stones in weight' because I was too over-weight to be a New Labour (women) candidate. The advice was from a member of Millbank staff. My reaction was 'May I have a word with you sister?' I had spent a lifetime in the Party campaigning for greater representation for women in the Party. I'm the last person that remark should have been made to.

ENCOUNTER TWO:

At the end of that session on handling the media I was told I was 'good at radio' and press releases to the papers. But I was also told that 'my attitude problem' came over on TV. I had departed from the message from time to time and, as a result, I could never represent the Party on TV!

When I asked if the candidates could give feedback on the weekend training session I was told this was 'not appropriate'. At the time, I was working in management training as a fully qualified trainer. The response to my question was delivered by one of the Millbank Mafia with a look of shock and surprise on their face. Clearly, questioning them in their performance was not allowed!

After this weekend I was not invited to any more sessions on 'presentation skills'.

ENCOUNTER THREE:

The same Millbank female accompanied a well turned out woman candidate during a walkabout in her prospective constituency in the company of a Shadow Minister. At one point she hissed at the candidate 'more lipstick – more lipstick!'

These incidents are by no means isolated ones. Another woman Labour MP for a Northern seat was complimented on her appearance and her media friendliness after she had undergone her radio and television mock interviews. But she was also banned by Millbank from ever representing the Party in the media. Her 'attitude problem' showed. Her 'attitude' is precisely that of a generation of women Labour politicians exemplified by the splendid Jo Richardson.

MPs can be banned only from broadcasts where an official line is needed. Broadcasters often ask the Party to 'put someone up' for interviews. But Millbank cannot silence MPs from all interviews. The Northern MP later appeared in a memorable radio interview along with an on-message sister (with views delicately manicured by Millbank) who tried to excoriate her for attacking and undermining New Labour policies.

The on-message MP was so gratuitously aggressive that she lost the mpathy of the listening audience. She annoyed the interviewer as ell. At the end of the item he kindly explained that the on-message P had angrily flounced 'out of the studio'. The debate was about cial security. The MP that Millbank said had unfortunate 'attitude' was e authentic voice of the great majority of rank and file Party mem-rs – especially women members.

Joan Ruddock MP was treated shamefully as Minister for Women. here was no salary as all the money had been used paying the boys. e was unceremoniously and unjustly dumped and the job was bolted to the already major one being done by Baroness Jay.

One of the shock losers at the Llanelli Assembly election, Ann rrard, was seen to shed a few tears on learning of her defeat. After all, t's how normal human beings behave. Immediately, her pager went . It was a female Labour Party Wales press person telling her to pull rself together because she was 'on television'. A male Labour MP in rdiff some years ago was allowed a full blown sob, undisturbed, when lost his seat. But that was before the days of control freakery.

Two newly ennobled top officials of the Labour Party recently toured bour's boilerhouse of (New) Millbank. They described their tour as e visiting an alien planet'. It was filled with strangers. Only two of staff were recognised as survivors from the Walworth Road days. The in function of the new staff appeared to them to be fund raising – ecially from major donors. Apparently they are very good at it.

But that is not a prime function of a political Party. Millbank is oked on the canard that electoral victory can be bought by the high-spender. It cannot. If they checked their calculations on the Euro-ction spending they will find that their faith is mis-placed. One raordinary wasteful, self-defeating, semi-legal jape was when Labour Wales tried some sleaze-in reverse. Instead of accepting lavish hospi-ty from big business bosses and lobbyists, Labour provided it.

A breakfast meeting, paid for by New Labour, was urged by Gordon own to love Labour and the Euro and to stuff Plaid. It was not one Gordon's most glorious moments.

This government has solid, major achievements to its name. It is suc-sfully following a populist role that will guarantee a long period in wer. The Tories are lost in limbo. Their Leader's absurd pitch to rouse rabble is, 'What do we want?'....Revolution! 'When do we want .... Now! 'What are we fighting for?'....Common sense?

Those with ambition are joining Labour. We are successful pub[lic] relations persuaders with an appeal that is sufficiently anaemic to [be] acceptable to the lowest common denominator of public acquiescen[ce] and prejudice.

Power politics have deluded New Labour. The Welsh stitch-ups a[re] the result of a creed that says that the core principles of democracy a[nd] anti-discrimination can be sacrificed to expediency: that loved val[ues] can be mocked and desecrated in the cause of petty advantage.

This process could devour the precious idealism that was our orig[i]nal inspiration and remains our vocation.

THE MIDDLE HERESY

'The far Left and the far Right have much in common'
Simon Hoggart.

PUBLIC IS GOOD: private is bad.

That was Labour's creed. Tories believed the opposite. Now we have stumbled on a new folly. Only a combination of the public and private will do. It is the absurd heresy of the Third Way.

Common sense proves that many problems are best solved by public solutions alone, others by private and some by a combination of both. The Third Way is what Bob Marshall-Andrews MP describes as the 'myth of the radical centre'.

British people ... will finally be allowed to inhabit a serene, unchallenged political landscape, rendered featureless by the soft climate of consensus and compromise. In this political never-never-land New Labour will not grow old and policy forums will debate endlessly the desiderata of government, blinded to their own impotence by the veil of flattered self-regard.

In the space between public and private blossom many winning strategies. The most prosperous future for the state enterprises of the Patent Office and the Post Office is to be liberated from stultifying Treasury rules. Then they can revel in the profits of entrepreneurial innovation while still clutching the family silver.

But liberation from one narrow dogma should not enslave us to another. Private Finance Initiatives (PFIs), Stakeholder Pensions and ISAs are Third Way solutions that could be best done by the public sector alone.

The trench war between Labour and big business was futile and damaging. We needed to get into bed with them. But surely it is going too far to allow them to consummate the relationship?

The Private Finance Initiative, like all cure-alls, is a deception. The new cash is very expensive money on which a huge price must be paid in future interest payments. But it is instant gratification for politicians – obtaining goodies today by paying twice for them tomorrow. But even worse is that many NHS hospitals and other services will slip into the control of private operators. Their service to the sick will then be secondary to their need to make profits. PFI may well turn out to mean Privatisation From Inside.

Gordon Brown is at his most self-righteous with his mantra that Labour does not spend what we have not earned. Except with PFI Francis Wheen in the Guardian has described how it works:

A project to rebuild University College Hospital, London, will 'save' £160m in capital costs by using PFI, but for the next 30 years the hospital trust will have to shell out almost £30m a year to the developer. In other words, the taxpayer is obliged to pay nearly £900m for something that would otherwise have cost £160. And, at the end of those 3 years, the hospital will belong to the private consortium. It's like taking out a mortgage from a loan shark to buy a house which you already own – and then discovering, 25 years down the line, that the property has been repossessed by the lender anyway.

Will today's Labour government be saying, 'Sorry, grandchildren we've shrunk the health service'?

Labour clearly had to dump much of the baggage that has kept the Party out of office for all but 24 years of this century. But so much disappeared in the Third Way clear out, we arrived in port with a vessel that was almost empty. By forgetting Labour's greatest achievements we threw some of the treasure chests overboard.

The quickest way to empty the Chamber of the Commons or to see the eyes of journalists glazing over is to mention pensions policy. Two issues dominated my campaigning life in 1999. One went nuclear, the other went phut. Mortgage mis-selling became a major national neurosis. A petition with 120,000 names calling for a better basic pension July 1999 went completely unnoticed. All journalists have mortgages None survive on a basic pension.

Forgotten by today's Parliament is that one supreme achievement our Party, the 1975 Pension Act. The long years of destruction followed Twenty years of salami cuts in the value of the basic pension now cheat ten million people out of over £1,000 a year.

Four MPs, led by Chris Mullin, once proposed a link between the el of the basic pension and the pay of MPs. Had it been successful, it ould certainly have concentrated the attention of MPs on the neg-cted issue of the annual scam of below-inflation increases in the basic nsion.

Sadly, Parliament has forgotten the example of the mis-selling of pri-te pensions and the roller coaster of annuity rates values that reveal ivate pensions as a rash gamble. Yet the state pension plus SERPS con-uued to deliver great value benefits at a tiny fraction of the adminis-tive costs of the morass of private, wastefully competitive schemes. ERPS is now to be abolished despite manifesto pledge to retain it. The perative of the new dogma produces a Third Way that borrows heav-from the follies of the private sector.

The overwhelming message of the Transport Select Committee that erved on in opposition from 92 to 97 was that privatisation of the lways was doctrinaire folly and dangerous. Labour in office forgot this essage until the Padding ton disaster. Privatisation of the railways was lerated because it fitted comfortably into the Middle Heresy of the ird Way.

The cerebral Tony Wright MP, a New Labour enthusiast, explained ny he fell out with fellow devotee of the creed, focus group guru ilip Gould. Writing about critics of New Labour's Freedom of formation proposals, Gould said 'I am certain the critics are wrong'. right replied:

How could he be certain the critics were wrong? As no arguments ere given, there was no way of knowing. What he was clearly certain out was that the the critics had to be wrong - necessarily, by defini-n - because otherwise the proposals might be flawed, which in terms his general argument about the radical, modernising credentials of ew Labour, was obviously impossible. Not only on this issue, but pre-mably on every other issue, there could therefore be no room for gitimate argument.

New Labour: Old Dogmatism. There is a political coterie who are dicted to the comfort blanket of dogma. They move comfortably m one extreme to the other. The rabid right-wing journalist Peter tchens found his present Tebbitt-admiring convictions a nanosecond er abandoning the Socialist Workers Party. Many New Labour apos-s spent their formative years in extreme left-wing groups. Peter andelson and many present Ministers and MPs are children of the revolutionary left.

The leap across the political spectrum can be made with deep-seate
attitudes intact. The absolute certainty of their views remain, so does a
intolerance of others, authoritarianism and an irritation with any cha
lenge to or deviation from a received verity. Once, all the enemies wel
'capitalists'. Now, all enemies are branded as forces of 'evil conse
vatism', i.e. all opponents of New Labour.

Labour Conferences now have the revivalist spirit of Moonie cor
ventions. When Eric Heffer was Chair in the early eighties, Conferenc
suffered an endless succession of hand-chop gesturing youths shriekir
Militant slogans in Liverpool accents. Now, a queue of well-dresse
holograms politely chant the Third Way nostrums. The conclusions ai
different, but in both Conferences there is little room for reason, debal
or argument.

John Major described Thatcher's slammed door closed mind. It's
contagion that afflicts this government. Rational thought is outlawed o
most subjects, most foolishly on illegal drugs. Although prohibition car
not work, no other policy can be considered. It's not working, so w
won't fix it. Thirty years of anti-drugs education has not reduce
America's drug problems. But Swiss and Dutch governments have ci
drugs deaths and crime. So Labour insists on repeating our anti-drug
failed policies instead of imitating Dutch successes.

Enforcer Cunningham explained why in his final frontbench appea
ance:

Labour Backbencher: Is there an example of an anti-drugs educatic
programme in this country or in any other country, in this century c
in any other century, that has led to a reduction in drug use?

Dr. Cunningham: Because things have not worked in the past, n
friend concludes that nothing can work in the future. I do not share th
pessimism.

'Continuing to do the same thing and expecting to get a differe
result' is the definition of madness (Rule N) given by Alcoholi
Anonymous to drunks who boast that they have learned to mana
their boozing .

Not pessimism Doctor Cunningham, madness.

WHY?

'I shall be an Autocrat, that's my trade. And the good Lord will forgive me, that's His.'

Catherine the Great

THE QUESTION that still baffles the Labour Party in Wales is what WAS all about?

The legacy of these awful months is a wreckage of dishonoured prin-ples, friendships ruptured, careers ruined or killed at birth, deep mis-ust and new, avoidable enmities. Some of the best in the Party are dis-lusioned and have gone. Others will soldier on with little conviction r hope.

The bedrock of our faith in the Labour Party was the certainty that e possess superior ideals and principles to all other Parties. Can this ill be true after the Party itself has trampled down our cherished val-es?

The plot to elect Alun has worked. This mess is the result of a 'suc-ss' in New Labour terms. The wild, dangerous gamble that Alun ould succeed as Leader could easily have ended in humiliation for him d for Tony Blair. If even one of the stitch-ups had failed, or one more ajor Union had voted democratically, the Downing Street plot would ve been killed off and Rhodri would be Leader.

Someone gambled that the risk was worthwhile. Who? Why? There as a Plan B. Some worried insiders forecast defeat for Alun and argued at the fight was not worth the candle. A plausible strategy was in place r Alun to withdraw gracefully and allow Rhodri to be the the only ndidate. Polling advice to some of those in the Alun-loop indicated at this would be a wise move. But there was an odd reaction. The poll ures were suppressed, even from some trusted allies of Alun. The word the one street that mattered was that 'Alun must not be allowed to lose'.

My own unhappiness with New Labour began in a fierce row wi
Tony Blair some four years ago. The Tories criticised him for saying o
thing and doing another – especially with his choice of school for l
son. His defence was unconvincing. But he was trapped when Harr
Harman committed a mortal sin to trump his venal one. Her child w
to go to a grammar school.

Blair had talked about not buckling to the pressure of 'political co
rectness'. Harriet spoke of the Iron Law of parenting: getting the b
for her children.

At a meeting of the Parliamentary Labour Party I read out an extra
from a letter a 77 year old constituent of mine sent to Harriet.

Surely you should know that getting special privileges for your s
was a gift to the Tory camp. Why are the hopes and aspirations of m
lions of ordinary folk secondary to the short term advantages of yo
family ?

I suggested to Harriet that one of the Iron Laws of Labour was n
to secure the best for your children at the price of depriving other ch
dren. I told Tony 'It's fine not to buckle, when you're right, but it
mulish stubbornness to do so when you're wrong'. I asked the
whether the inner circle had lost touch, 'isolated in a golden circle
beautiful people, bound together with ties of mutual admiration arou
their leader'.

In reply, Blair said he would stand by Harriet. He could not sack b
without exposing himself. She should have resigned. Frustrated abo
what was happening, I wrote a letter to the Guardian in code that w
impenetrable except to a few. They published it under the ti
'Midwitch Socialists':

I have a nightmare. If an alien force wishes to take over a count
they could grow foreign beings in veal crates in public schools, feedi
them a special diet that made them beautiful and ambitious, but stu
ed their idealism. They then would be placed as an incubus inside
political Party who would love and reward them with applause a
high office. Sometimes the deception would falter, on an issue such
school choice, and the Party may suspect that these beings are alien
in the Party, but not of the Party. Too late, the Midwitch Socialists wo
get so strong that they would destroy their host Party.

But it's only a nightmare, isn't it ?

Discerning fellow MPs said it was no joke. Our Party was being colonised by a non-Labour succubus. That nightmare has haunted many of us since. On reflection, Tony Blair may ask himself why he sacrificed so much to keep Harriet. The row gave the Tories their deadliest ammunition. Harriet's Ministerial career was barren and brief. Does Tony's loyalty to old friends override his common sense? A possible explanation of his suicidal strategy in Wales is his unreasonable, voracious loyalty to his friend Alun.

If so, why not a share of loyalty to Rhodri who was appointed to frontbench roles by three Labour leaders? Outsiders may start to believe that Rhodri would have been inadequate, that there is some serious problem with him known only to Downing Street, possibly a fault even more heinous than his reluctance to plump up cushions.

I have spent many years of my life working with Alun and Rhodri. For five years I shared an office with both of them and a flat with one of them for 11 years. I spent a holiday with Rhodri and our wives, romping across Iceland. We all remained on friendly terms even at the end of that. I know both of them very well. Rhodri would have been a different leader to Alun. In my view he would have been far superior. But both of them are fine gifted men and skilful politicians.

So why was the battle worthwhile? Why did New Labour back a candidate who was so unpopular and unconvincing? Towards the end of the Leadership campaign, on February 12, a poll showed that Alun had lamentably failed to win public support. Only 16% of the General Public backed him compared with 55% backing Rhodri. The electoral calamity of May 6th was guaranteed.

This is an irritating puzzle The basic tenet of New Labour is that, electoral success is the supreme god to which all else should be sacrificed. Here chicanery had produced a leader guaranteed to scuttle chances of a Labour electoral majority. Why?

There are a number of possible explanations. One is the need of the Leadership of the Party to control every activity in minute detail. It is a version of Democratic Centralism, practised with tedious regimentation by far-left sects. Must it be that one person's will must dominate every decision, regardless of the destruction that results? If that is so, it has profound implications for the future of New Labour.

Another explanation is found in Downing Street's weak commitment to devolution. They need someone in charge on Cardiff Bay who can

be controlled, to restrict devolved powers – devolution but not divorc
In that respect, there is a difference between the two men. Alun w
happily do the bidding of Tony Blair, partly because he identifies clos
ly with him and partly because of his submissive personality. Rhod
will veer away from central control when he believes that it is in the be
interest of Wales. If that is so, it explains the Devo-droop revealed belo

An astute observer answered my invitation on the future of the Par
with this bleak but accurate analysis:

I find that there is very little energy or interest within the Party
developing devolution. There is little new thinking either within
outside the Party. There is virtually no debate about what devolutic
entails for the Party in Wales or what our policy programme should b
What is our vision of what a devolved Wales will look like? It may b
that Party members feel shell-shocked or uninvolved with the Par
after the Blairite 'reforms'. There is a conformist culture in the Wel
Party which is largely anti-intellectual and uncomfortable with debat
But this may just mirror the flabby intellectual life in Wales general
which is content to put up with a rather cozy and complacent conse:
sus.

Throughout the Leadership campaign, it was repeatedly claimed,
Tony Blair and others, that the electoral college being used to elect Al
as Leader was the same as that used to elect Tony. But there was a cr
cial difference which has never been admitted. As recently as July, a to
official of the party was still emphatically repeating this untruth, to
meeting of MPs. In August, I wrote to the General Secretary of tl
Party:

In the interest of accuracy I would invite your comment on the clai
that will appear in two forthcoming books, i.e. that the electoral cc
lege system was different in the Michael-Morgan election to that us
in the 1994 Blair Leadership election. The Unions were then told th
unless they had Omov ballots they would not be allowed to vote
understand that UCATT did not comply and were not allowed to ta
part. If you disagree with this, please let me know.

No reply was received. It's called being in denial.

DEVO-DROOP

'A penny off Income Tax hypothecated to education is hardly the battle Hymn of the Republic'
Bob Marshall Andrews MP.

DEVOLUTION is in serious trouble. Westminster has declared it to be an event – not a process.

Alun and Rhodri have put aside their antagonisms and welded the majority of the AMs into an increasingly coherent team. The Assembly must be allowed a period to settle in before we can reasonably expect them to deliver. There are some hopeful trends. The Welsh Assembly has dumped the verbal junk that clogs the Westminster Parliament. Use of Welsh is natural and without problems.

There have been few policy differences with Westminster. The Assembly caved in to the most skilful and persistent lobby of the farmers. Nick Brown told the farmers that over-production was their fault. The farm Unions used animal abuse, animal welfare, blackmail and half-truths against the AMs. The Assembly ignominiously surrendered and promised cash aid without knowing which other service would be robbed to provide it.

A Wales-only solution promised the horror of English drovers herding their flocks across the borders to harvest subsidies. The government then caved in. The volte face may indicate an unexpected role for the Assembly. It could either be a lever for forcing UK action, or a weak link that breaks rational but unpopular policies. Most AMs are political virgins who have prove susceptible to the heady blandishments of the political persuaders. The lobbyists will have scented the weakness and will plague AMs with pleas for favours for their rich clients.

The original infestation of lobbyists has not found Cardiff to be an agreeable habitat. Lobbying is the mother of corruption and they should be shown the door. By lying down and letting the farmers walk all ov them, the AMs have invited the lobbyists back.

An unexpected result of the stitch-up has been to rob Labour of i overall majority. It was universally accepted wisdom that Labour AM would outnumber those of all other parties and form a majority gov ernment. Not until the final days of the election did anyone dare sug gest any other possibility. Labour and Tony Blair were still popular in th UK and the polls continue to reassure.

The rules of the Assembly were designed to give minority Parti strong voices and a share in power. 'Inclusive' was the word overused the planning of the Wales Act and by the committee that finalised th rules. They planned to avoid the horror of permanent one-Party dom inance – a Glamorgan County Council on stilts. The right of Plaid, To and Lib Dem AMs to share decision-making was carefully crafted in the Assembly's procedures.

But the minority Parties do not need any positive discrimination. T result is a weak Assembly. Labour's 28 seat group is three short of overall majority. Wrexham's John Marek has been accused by To Leader Nick Bourne of forming his own Party. He has threatened take a line which is independent of the Labour Group. Jane Davidson deputy Presiding Officer and does not vote. Ron Davies is brooding c the sidelines, tossing the odd wounding dart here and there.

The Labour group can guarantee to muster only 25 votes against th combined strength of the opposition parties (minus the Presidin Officer) of 31. Any decision of the group can be overthrown by th Assembly. Alun squared up to the farmers, then he was squashed by th might of the combined steamroller of the opposition Parties. Procedur designed to protect small Parties have enfeebled the majority Party.

In October the steamroller of a vote of censure squashed agricultu al secretary Christine Gwyther. Alun Michael again defied democra and announced that christine would stay in post. The Wesrern M howled. The habit of power was so deeply ingrained in the Labour Par in South Wales a mere majority vote by elected AM's was brushed asi as an irritating irrelevance. Even a pretence at democracy was not trie

More squawking chickens came home to roost in October. The b for the timid treatment of Rhondda Cynon Taff Council and other los making during the leadership and Elections was delivered. Th Assembly Cabinet provokedopen revolt by approving an extra coun tax chrage of £50 per household throughout Wales to bail out the loss makers

The North Wales daily Post headlined the £50 rise per family that every North Walian family would have to fork out to rescue the four South Wales councils. Council taxpayers in Newport were already rebellious. The previous year they paid a 15% hike in council tax bills largely to pay for expensive services in Valley areas out of control of their local councillors.

At a meeting of the Partnership commitee between the Assembly and Council leaders Newport's Herry Jones said:

> *'It is time these four got their service provision right. Why should 18 authorities subsidise four others which have done absolutely nothing to bring their services into line?'*

The inactivity of the Welsh Office under Alun Michael had proved a disincentive to improvements in efficiency by the four local councils. Was he disabled earlier in the year bt the paramount need to secure the backing of trade unions and council bosses to tighten the stitch up of his own election?

No help is on hand from the architect of devolution. Ron Davies has been exiled to the backbenches where his talents will be underused. Another spell of 'bird watching' was reported by the News of the World. The allegations were detailed and spread over five days. One of the days in which alleged questionable behaviour took place was the day of the European Election. Ron denied the stories.

In spite of the paper's exaggerated claims, the allegations were not supported by photographs that showed anything of significance. Not for the last time, the News of the World was building on an accepted perception of scandal. But to his fellow AMs, this was an allegation too far. He has since revealed that he is undergoing psychiatric counselling for his difficulties.

The 'Ron' issue has dominated Assembly life. The debates are less than thrilling. Some AMs read oral questions from a sedentary position. Why not just fax them in? It was also wrong of Alun to defend an AM who refused to give way in mid-speech. Many dead Parliaments allow MPs to drone on endlessly without interruption. Interventions are the spice of debates.

There were some early grounds for optimism that the aim of Welsh solutions for Welsh problems could become more than a slogan, that the Welsh Labour Party could liberate itself from the centralism of Millbank and Downing Street. Those hopes are now as dim as a dying glow worm.

Downing Street has clamped down on any strengthening of devolved powers. Strongly devolutionist Ministers, Jon Owen Jones and Calum MacDonald were sacked from their respective Welsh and Scottish jobs in July. Calum's replacement is Brian Wilson who, apart from Tam Dalyell, is the most virulently anti-devolutionist of all Scots Labour MPs.

New Welsh Secretary Paul Murphy was a reluctant convert to a weak brew of devolution when he was a Shadow Welsh Office Minister. In 1979 he was a principal officer of the Welsh campaign against devolution. He was supported enthusiastically then, as now, by Don Touhig.

As the new Welsh Field Marshal, he tried to rally his army at the Bournemouth Conference in September 1999 with a unique battle cry. It was not 'Forward to battle, troops! ' or even 'Full Retreat!'. Rather, it was, 'Stay exactly where you are'. He described the present wretched, weak and unstable Welsh devolution as 'settled'.

An MP once did a party charade in which he invited others to guess 'Who am I?' He then opened and closed his mouth like a goldfish, shifted from one foot to the other while gazing at the ceiling. The answer to this conundrum was 'Paul Murphy, singing the Welsh National Anthem'.

Paul's antagonism to the Welsh language is not skin deep. He share with MPs Alan Williams (Swansea West) and Llew Smith a tribal phobia of Welsh. Perhaps his high office will change Paul. He did a splendid job in Northern Ireland where his sincere devout Catholicism wa no impediment in his work with all denominations. He earned the respect of all sides.

At Bournemouth, Paul said 'Together we reflect the wishes of the people of Wales who voted to have an Assembly and also voted to be part of the United Kingdom'. In a letter to the Western Mail, Hamish Richards responded:

That is not true. The referendum was limited to the issue of an Assembly. It was a straightforward Yes or No vote. The Parliament for Wales Campaign had advocated a 'multiple choice' referendum which could have shown whether or not there was a desire to have the weak Assembly on offer; one with powers similar to those being at the time offered to Scotland; one as part of a UK Federal system of government; or independence. The Labour Party would have nothing to do with such an idea. Only a Yes/No option was put to the voters. How then can Paul Murphy say that the people of Wales have voted to be part of the United Kingdom?

The authentic voice of old Labourism was heard in the conference at Bournemouth. Labourism had ruled much of South Wales for a century. Now to be confused with the 'True labour" that Rhodri exemplifies, Labourism was backward-looking and self-serving. The legacy has been one of intolerance and dictatorship. One of the very few delegates selected to speak at Bournemouth was veteran valley party potentate Ken Hopkins. He has moved effortlessly from autocratic Labourism to autocratic New Labour without disturbing a brain cell.. He weakly echoed Paul Murphy's plea not to allow Wales any more power, bashed the Nats. and then sang a song. One delegate said his grovellingly servile speech made her feel 'ashamed to be Welsh.'

Also favoured with a call to the rostrum was Terry Thomas. His view seems to be that it is fine to be a puppet because that gave Wales a minimum wage. In 1979 Wales became the first nation in the world to reject a greater say in running our own affairs. In Bournemouth, Alun, Paul Murphy, Ken Hopkins and Terry Thomas all pleaded that Wales should have no more devolved powers. This is not showing the best feature of our country. It was Wales mooning at the the British Labour Party.

Blair has stamped on the brakes and the chocks have hammered under the wheels of devolution. Elsewhere in the world, nations which have had a taste of self-rule demand more. New tensions are now certain between centralising Blairism and the devolutionary forces of all Welsh Parties. The nature of all institutions is to seek greater powers for themselves. Even the Tories will be infected by institutionalitis. They will refuse to plot their own demise and come to love devolution. The Assembly itself, even under Alun's leadership, is unlikely to conspire with Blair in debilitating its own stature and influence.

Labour could be sowing the seeds of future electoral problems. With the sole exception of the Italian Communist Party, all major opposition parties in Europe this century have had their turn in government. The nationalists will mount serious challenges to Labour in Scotland and

Wales in future elections. The next Assembly election is likely to be held when Labour is at the half-way mark of its second term of government at Westminster.

The nationalists will be armed with the populist, persuasive cry of 'more power to our nation'. Will Labour stir the passions of voters with a summons to 'stand still'. Will voters be aroused by the affirmation that the perfect New Jerusalem has already been built on Cardiff Bay?

Labour Assembly Members are discomfited by their minority role. Several are ex-Councillors long used to exercising permanent Labour power. Richard Edwards, AM for Preseli Pembrokeshire, has no regrets about Labour's command of the political high ground by our adoption of PR for the Welsh General Election. But that advantage has been lost. He told a fringe meeting at Bournemouth that the 'genetically modified' leadership rules were at fault. 'I'm not talking about Blair', he said. 'This little Frankenstein was made in Wales and made by the Wales Labour Executive'.

The habitat of Labour in Wales for a century has been the moral high ground. It's time for us to return home.

Resurgence ?

A lot of things that many of us have said in the past three years are going to be unsaid'

Denis Healey 1968

ONE OF THE MOST eloquent responses to the web edition of this book was the silence of the establishment of the Party in Wales. Monosyllabic comments had to be yanked out of them by persistent journalists.

They wanted to run home, hide their heads under the pillow and pretend that the events of the past year never happened. The other alternative was to wash the memory out of their heads with a cocktail of rhetoric and make believe at the Bournemouth Conference.

The solutions are not easy. There can be no shackling together of all elements of the Welsh Party by mere appeals for unity, particularly when those calls come from the perpetrators of the dishonourable machinations of the past twelve months. The attempts to fictionalise the severity of the chicanery must be exposed. The fixes, the deceptions and the abuses of authority were far more heinous than previously believed.

Many have benefited. Others may well be rewarded in future for their roles, with jobs and honours. One correspondent has suggested that I add a blank pages to this book entitled 'The Wages of Sin', so readers can write in the honours, jobs, peerages and patronage that are bestowed on those who orchestrated the stitch-ups or collaborated with them.

However, Labour Party Wales is being rejuvenated. Jessica Morden is the 30 year old new broom as General Secretary. She is highly intelligent, resourceful and well respected. The enforced reaction of the Welsh Labour Party office to the web edition of this book was restrained but incontrovertably true. The official spokesperson said 'Paul is Paul'.

There is no agreed blueprint on the way forward. The warfare among Welsh Labour MPs has paused with a unanimous vote for the critical report on the Assembly elections. Rhodri has been magnanimous in defeat and has thrown himself wholeheartedly into a secondary role at the Assembly. He is loyal to Alun and the institution and has put aside the understandable rancour he may feel. This book has been prepared without his knowledge or approval. I have not approached him or Alun Michael about its publication. They have had the chance to read it on. Neither has responded.

A new group has been formed within the party in Wales. Its title is the Welsh word for opportunity, CYFLE. The acronym is based on its aim in English – Campaigning for Your Franchise on the Labour Executive. The list of supporters is impressive and reflects the widespread discontent with the fix.

The initial supporters include MPs Martin Caton, Jackie Lawrence, Julie Morgan, Ann Clwyd and Rhodri Morgan plus MEP Eluned Morgan. Twelve Assembly Members are backers, including Cabinet members Jane Hutt, Chris Gwyther and Andrew Davies.

CYFLE described the past year as 'Among the worst in the history of the Wales Labour Party'. Their remedy is fair representation of members on the Executive, elected by Omov and fully accountable to their electors.

CYFLE is taken seriously enough to have been mildly rebuked by MEP supporter Eluned Morgan. She suggested that there was 'nothing to be gained from staging a re-run of the Leadership election'. Nobody wants to endure that nightmare again. Alun is very comfortably ensconced in his majestic office. It commands splendid views over Cardiff Bay and almost the entire area of his Cardiff South and Penarth constituency. Cardiff Bay, for which he fought and suffered in Parliament, will soon be beautiful, filled with a vast lake of reflective water. It would take nothing less a platoon of the SAS to eject Alun from his office.

There are ways to create democratic structures in the Welsh party and to win back confidence. Cardiff Councillor and Rhodri supporter Kevin Brennan urged the use of existing mail shots to members for ballots and to raise some ethical sponsorship. These are sound practical steps to rebuild the party.

Richards Edwards AM has said that, eight months after the February fix, 'Party morale is at a low ebb. We have a minority Labour administration that is at the mercy of the opposition's whim and fancy.' Cardiff

North MP Julie Morgan warned after a summer of doorstep campaigning that discontent with the way the party handled the leadership is still coming up at the doorstep. 'We've not yet re-established trust with the people'.

The fixers, the fiddlers and the cheats damaged Labour's good name. They are now trying to silence the messengers. We cannot come to terms with the truth until we first confront it. Only then can we win back the respect of the people of Wales. To be silent after this awful year is not a choice.

There is a sincere, deeply felt need to unite and re-build. In Wales, Labour's schizophrenia on home-rule has continued for a full century. Keir Hardie was an enthusiast: other genuine comrades believe it is a distraction and a trap. Wales has a long, precious radical tradition. Ted Rowlands has said that the Labour Party in Wales is rooted in 'old' Labour values. A whole generation of Welsh politicians has been brushed aside because of ageism and because Welsh ideals do not fit perfectly into the New Labour jig-saw.

We do not have to suffer the waste of the Middle Heresy. If the majority in the Assembly were the natural heirs to our Welsh traditions, government would be far more radical and progressive. There is little hope of that if remote control by Millbank operates. The spirit of Aneurin Bevan binds the party together in Wales. He said that he thought there is an argument for devolution of power. He told the Westminster Parliament:

Wales has a special place, a special individuality, a special culture and special claims, and I do not think that this is the place where any of them can properly be considered.

Now, we have a better place.

VOX NET

ON 15 SEPTEMBER 1999, when the first version of this book was put on the Internet, 15,017 hits were recorded on my web-site. Over the next three days a further 18,000 hits were counted.

In the web version, I said that 'All are now invited to add their views. The final version of this book will be shaped by submissions received. Some of my conclusions may be reinforced or contradicted, inferences may be strengthened or denied, additional stitch-ups may come to light, or benign explanations of those already identified may be offered'.

A shoal of e-mails arrived. Many of their messages have now been incorporated into the text. Others could not be. Some were malicious to the personae of the drama. Others cannot be used because they breached confidences and would identify my informants. The possibility of writs has inhibited my publishing other disturbing facts. In an interview about the web version, I said that I had been told that I had knowledge of 70% of the stitch-ups. Information has arrived on the other 30%. Regrettably, much of it is unpublishable at the moment. But it all strengthens my conviction that this book is essential for the future good health of the Labour Party, particularly in Wales.

As far as I know, this is the first experiment in publishing a book in two stages in this way. It provides an opportunity for second thoughts. Many changes have been made from the original account based on the fresh information and argument that have been flown in through cyberspace.

Only one correspondent was against the publication of the book. Others have expressed unhappiness with some versions of events that were sent to them before publication. In those instances, where I was convinced of possible unfairness or inaccuracies, I have withdrawn items.

The following are a representative cross-section of replies, printed in the languages in which they were sent:

I can not let your view of the Assembly's opening pass without comment.

Either your irony slipped past me or you were at a different event. The opening of the Assembly was instantly forgettable. A low budget half hearted shambles. An embarrassing concert at the pier head rounded off a dismal day.

Tired celebrities, tired performers watched by tired people. What a way to start a new political beginning. Only the fireworks were worth watching.

Compared with the 'Scottish Event' a proper opening in a proud capital of a proper Parliament..well it will be soon. Having watched our AMs perform on daytime TV what an uninspiring bunch of hacks and no hopers.

Stay in Westminster Paul, Wales needs you there at the heart until either the Assembly collapses under its own weight of inertia or the people of Wales wake up and demand a Parliament of their own. Phew, glad to get that off my chest,

* * *

My perception of Ron Davies, prior to the headlines, was that the Welsh public would have benefited from him not being the leader of Labour in Wales. He just didn't seem to be doing a good job of it, at all, a fact everyone I spoke to about it agreed on. He simply wasn't popular.

Conversely, I have no problems with the conduct of Peter Hain. I've read that he's a bit of a political salamander, but I thought he was outstanding during the Assembly referendum. As I recall Neath and Port Talbot had the largest majority for the Assembly of any region in Wales, and I'm afraid that simply does not happen by accident. I saw him pounding the streets of Neath for hours before the vote.

As for Alun Michael's, I think it's generally regarded that he's a Westminster stooge, but I didn't particularly want to see Rhodri Morgan in his place either. This is partially due to Rhodri campaigning for Cardiff against Swansea for the Assembly location (the people of Cardiff made it pretty clear they couldn't give a toss about the Assembly with their referendum vote, so why should that have the pleasure of hosting it by default?), but I didn't know enough about the guy to approve.

However it was very clear that between Alun and Rhodri there was only one democratic winner. But since when did incumbent politics have anything to do with democracy?

By the way, excellent use of technology. Glad to see a Welshman pushing the envelope.

* * *

Pub hwyl gyda lansio'r llyfr! Rwyn arbennig o falch eich bod chi wedi ysgrifennu'r llyfr arbennig hwn!

Pob hwyl

* * *

Very witty Paul, I'm looking forward to increasing your profit margin. We won Islwyn (&Rhondda) because we were - young, willing & able (compared to...) A young and flexible Party of the people - and Wales!

Best of luck butty

* * *

Gwefan briliant - mae'n gret i weld aelod seneddol sydd a hiwmor ac yn barod i ddweud ei farn am ei gyd aelodau. Mae ychydig o anarchi-aeth yn dda i ddemocrataeth. Mwy o nerth i'ch braich (a'ch gwefan!)

* * *

I am not happy with what is currently happening in Cardiff Bay. That, of course, can be attributed to two factors: first, the fall of Ron Davies and consequently the abandonment of the concept of devolution being a process and not an event and second the 'triumph' of Alun Michael with his lack of interest in the devolution process together with the fact that the better AM's on the Labour side lurk in the background while roles *have been given to the New Labour nonentities with which he has surrounded himself. What I long to see is the opposition parties getting together to bring down the present administration in a secret ballot which will also have the support of the half dozen or so 'real Labour' AM's. The opportunity for this can come on the 'Matching Funds' issue.*

I would like you to confine the award of 'flames' to the devolution issue. If you were to do that, there is no way you can give even one flame to Alun Michael.

On the morning after the Referendum result. There was a victory demonstration outside the Cardiff City Hall. I was in a small group that comprised the three Cardiff MP's Rhodri and Julie as well as Jon Owen Jones (but no Alun Michael - apparently he was not even in Cardiff). Wayne David was also there as was Bert Pierce, the former Secretary of the Communist Party in Wales. The main topic of conversation was that the people of Cardiff had produced a 'No' result. The three MP's felt this badly, given the tremendous effort they had each put into the 'Yes' campaign. They were convinced that if Alun Michael had also contributed to the Yes campaign, there could have been a different result in Cardiff . Alun Michael was not a popular colleague!! Clearly, he was not committed to devolution in 1997. I cannot comment on his claim that he was an avid supporter of devolution But I am convinced that such support would be the outcome of expediency rather than enthusiasm. So, please, only pom-poms for Alun!!

* * *

Don't you think the book will help only our political opponents, Paul? (From a Labour AM)

* * *

I've had a brief read and love it. I was a 'Child of Thatcher' but soon saw the light! What I've read so far is so very true. Keep up the good work and, as Michael Meacher said (in very different circumstances), 'don't let the b******s get you down'. Kind regards,

* * *

John Marek should have four flames as he was brilliant during the campaign He was the only MP in North Wales who was vocal in his support for Rhodri.

I am sure you gave his fifth flame to Don Touhig by mistake. I am pleased to see you changed his one flame to flickering but I do feel it should be extinguished immediately. George 'I believe in one man, one vote and that man is me' Wright should have no flames and five pom poms in my opinion!!

* * *

An amazingly honest book!!

I can't believe how true it all is in your description of the stitch-up. The only possible explanation must be to stop further Welsh devolution. But don't you think that going so public might make the stitchers dig their heels in now that they have been so comprehensively humiliated?

Wedi Darllen y bennod gyntaf ac yn edrych ymlaen at ddarllen y gweddill. Mae angen gwirioneddol am hanes o'r fath ac Rwy'n falch eich bod wedi mynd ati i gofnodi'r cyfnod allweddol hwn yn Hanes Cymru. Cefais flas mawr a 'Baglu Mlaen'.

* * *

(Several versions of the events described in the following e-mail have been received. I have no doubt that it is entirely true. In the interests of the caution, I have air-brushed out the names)

A good little illustration of the Union battle is the xxxx. In the local office there was a split. John X recently merged from another union wanted an Omov vote and backed Rhodri. John Z wanted to back Alun. A meeting of members narrowly voted for RM and John Z was instructed to cast the Union's ballot for Rhodri.

Subsequently however he claimed that eligibility to vote had not been properly checked at the meeting, and therefore the vote was invalid. A furious John X contacted the national office who had advised the branch to use Omov.

An instruction was issued that John Z should cast the vote for Rhodri and send a photocopy of the ballot paper to the union's HQ. By the last day for voting the ballot paper had still not arrived at Transport House. John X went there and was issued with a duplicate by Anita Gale and allowed to cast his vote for Rhodri - on hearing this news I knew that it was all over and we had definitely lost.

Have you thought of adding a section 'Where are they now' - i.e. The number of stitch-uppers with consultancies, places in the Lords, honours, jobs in the Assembly etc... This is a real concern.

Diddorol a difyrrus. Fydd y spin doctors ddim yn hapus; diolch byth mae guts gyda rhywun i ddweud y gwir.   Pob lwc gyda'r llyfr.

Ardderchog Paul, fel aelod Plaid Lafur mi fwynhais y safle gwe ac edrychaf ymlaen i brynu dy llyfr di newydd. Pob lwc i chwi.   Cofion gorau

I love the new book, it is so refreshing to see an MP actually doing what he was elected to do - keep it up!

I have often been struck by the difference between Scottish and Welsh institutions, (eg. Scottish and Welsh LP Executive Committees.) It is like the difference between, the 'old' Billy Connolly and Max Boyce - one is very assertive, even aggressive, confident and outgoing, the other more unconfident, rather sentimental and parochial. And in many ways these differences reflect deeper cultural difference.

APPENDIX

How the Unions Voted, or Otherwise ...

AEEU: 65,000 : 6.2% : Michael,
Delegates vote

GMB: 64,000: 6.2%: Michael,
A mystery. Not Omov

TGWU: 53,000: 5.1%: Michael
No Ballot.

UNISON: 53,000: 5.1%: Morgan
Omov Ballot.

CWU: 13,000: 1.2%: Morgan
Delegates.

FBU: 2,500: 0.2%: Morgan
Omov Ballot

GPMU: 5,000: 0.5%: Morgan
No Ballot.

ISTC: 10,300: 1%: Michael
No Ballot.

MSF: 11,000: 1%: Morgan.
Omov Ballot

NUM: 12,000: 1.1% Morgan
Omov Ballot.

TSSA: 1,000: 0.1%: Morgan.

UCATT: 4,000: 0.5%: Morgan.

USDAW: 19,000: 2%: Morgan
Delegates vote.

Aslef: 10,000: 1%: abstained.

Other Affiliated Bodies

Co-op Party: 19,000: 2pc: Michael.
Fabian: n/k: 0.1%: abstained.
Socialist Educ Assoc: n/k: 0.1pc: Morgan.
Wales Lab Students: 200: 0.1%: Michael.